A Guide to Prehistoric Sites
in Monmouthshire

Monuments in the Landscape

Volume IV

A Guide to Prehistoric Sites in Monmouthshire

by
George Children and George Nash

Logaston Press

LOGASTON PRESS
Little Logaston Woonton Almeley
Herefordshire HR3 6QH

First published by Logaston Press 1996
Copyright © George Children and George Nash 1996

ISBN 1 873827 49 0

Set in Times 11/13 pt by Logaston Press
and printed in Great Britain by The Cromwell Press, Melksham

This book is dedicated to John, Jude and Hannah
(Their bedrooms are sites as well)

Please Note

All the sites covered in this book are prehistoric. Many are pre-Bronze and Iron Age and therefore there is no metal present to be located by metal detectors. To protect certain Bronze and Iron Age sites, the authors have refrained from using detailed grid references, and in the case of Neolithic stray finds, only a four figure number has been used.

The following points must be observed:

1. Always follow the Countryside Code.

2. On all sites, extreme care should be taken.

3. Any artefacts found within the county should be reported to the Glamorgan-Gwent Archaeology Trust, Ferryside Warehouse, Bath Lane, Swansea SA1 1RD, or at any local museum.

4. Under no circumstances should visitors dig around or on any site. Any damage could result in prosecution.

5. It is an offence under the 1979 Ancient Monuments and Archaeological Areas Act to use metal detectors on or near scheduled ancient monuments. In addition, simple 'treasure hunting' near ancient monuments can well damage evidence to such an extent that archaeologists are unable to interpret it fully in the future.

Contents

Acknowledgments

Many of the ideas expressed in this volume derive from endless discussion and debate of what may be considered a limited literature. The authors' motivation for such a project was an opportunity for endless cups of tea (red label) and ravioli on toast (topped with cheese)—thank you Safeway!

Part of this book is dedicated to Edward Andrews Downman, a most competent surveyor and enthusiast who, between 1910 and 1914, surveyed and recorded many of the hillforts and later earthworks within the area that was then Monmouthshire. It is the oft-forgotten detailed records such as these that enhance our interpretation of the past.

The authors would like to thank the following for their help with this book. Sincere thanks go to Frank Olding (Curator of Abergavenny Museum), Jan Allen, Neil Nayling, Charles Hill (Glamorgan-Gwent Archaeological Trust), Sue Hamilton (University College, London), Jayne Pilkington (Museum of London Archaeology Service) and Jonathan Mullis (Babtie, Reading). Finally, a big thank you to Andy Johnson who took time to harass, edit and produce this, our second book for this series.

George & George
October 1996

Introduction

When writing this volume, the authors were initially concerned about the apparent limited number of sites. Not surprisingly, the farther one travels back in time, the more fragmentary and dispersed the evidence becomes. One problem we encountered was that many of the early Palaeolithic and Mesolithic sites were 'just across the border'. Indeed, we have included two cave sites which are but a few hundred metres inside Herefordshire—King Arthur's Cave and Merlin's Cave. Both sites were excavated during the latter part of the nineteenth and early part of the twentieth centuries and the finds from both caves, in particular from King Arthur's Cave were split into three parts. One third were deposited in Monmouth Museum. More detailed reasons for including these sites in this volume are set out in the main text, for it is important to understand that modern boundaries are often just artificial lines drawn across a landscape. One can see even today such changes with four new unitary authorities carved out of Gwent, itself a replacement for the Monmouthshire covered in this book. If we consider the past, both cave sites may have as much a legitimate right of being a part of Monmouthshire's prehistory as the Mesolithic footprints that are seen walking into the Severn Estuary near Caldicot.

Early prehistoric sites are limited, but they nonetheless establish a firm starting point on which to base this book. As we shall see, many sites developed over long periods of time—they become multi-phase monuments creating their own sense of history. More importantly, they give identity to people, the most important component to the archaeologist.

The chambered monuments of the Neolithic as well as the barrows, stone circles and standing stones of the Bronze Age are a testament to the complexity of socially and symbolically controlled landscapes and are the first monuments of Monmouthshire that are truly megalithic. These monuments humanise the landscape. The people of the Iron Age, with their hillforts and enclosures, created a similar effect on the landscape, albeit political and economic. We too, within our daily lives, create and recreate the landscape. The county of Monmouthshire is one of the most heavily industrially-scarred landscapes of Europe, with its own uniqueness. Similarly, the landscape in prehistoric times was scarred.

This book is itself an archaeological excavation, as it attempts to peel off layer by layer each period to reveal the prehistory of Monmouthshire. As you work through this book, we hope you will draw many comparisons between life then and now, for prehistoric people were essentially no different from ourselves; their aspirations, needs and desires were just as valid.

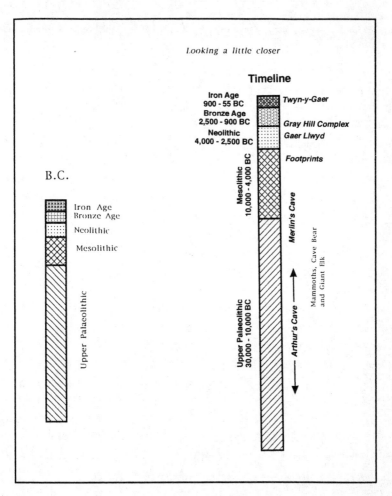

This timeline outlines a rigid series of periods. This is somewhat misleading, for in no case was change an 'overnight affair'. Many ideas, in particular those linked with burial, economy and the social fabric, would have been slow to take effect. So, although the timeline represents an accurate chronology, the reader should be aware that realtiy is not as clearcut as the diagram suggests. Many of the sites mentioned in this book cannot be assigned to one single period. For example, the cave sites on the Doward not only represent the Upper Palaeolithic but also the Mesolithic, the Roman period and even the recent industrial past.

The Stone Ages

What constitutes a landscape? Do we state the obvious and list mountains, hills, rivers, streams and trees? Can we include settlements, hillforts, burial monuments and caves? The way in which we, as individuals, look at landscape determines what we see. As archaeologists we try to comprehend the landscape as a whole, uniting both natural and artificial components. However we perceive it, there is no doubt that the landscape of Monmouthshire is naturally diverse and has, from the ancient to the recent past, been manipulated according to the resources that were economically, socially and symbolically available.

The early hunters: The Upper Palaeolithic

The perception and utilisation of Monmouthshire's landscape can be traced at least as far back as the Upper Palaeolithic period (35,000-10,000 BC), if not earlier. The southern and eastern lowlands of Monmouthshire (the Wentlooge and Caldicot Levels, collectively known as the Gwent Levels) then formed part of an extended plain stretching as far as present-day Somerset and north Devon.

It almost goes without saying that the further one travels back in time, the more tenuous the artefact evidence becomes and the available evidence for the Old Stone Age (the Palaeolithic) in Monmouthshire is, to say the least, limited. The evidence is dominated by flint and stone tools. The shape, size and function of these tools, although important, say very little about people. To paraphrase the historian, R.G. Collingwood, 'it is not knowing what people made but understanding what they thought that is the proper

1

definition of the archaeologist's task.' In order to put 'flesh on the bones' we must speculate and, more importantly, draw analogies from historical and contemporary sources where these exist. Obviously, we cannot be totally satisfied using these approaches, but by so doing it is possible to create a picture of the Old Stone Age that is both alive and meaningful.

The poor preservation of many artefacts from the period is a major problem. Very few organic remains such as mollusc shells, seeds and bone can survive ten, fifteen or twenty thousand years within the area's acidic soils, unless found in a cave or rock shelter. Within the county, evidence for the Upper Palaeolithic is concentrated in clusters of finds which have been unearthed due to recent town and city development. This clustering probably provides a distorted account of the period. Fortunately, along the rivers Wye and Severn on the western and northern borders of Monmouthshire, there is a series of caves and rock shelters which, over the past twenty years, has revealed a fragmented picture of the distant past. Recent investigations, mainly in neighbouring Herefordshire, have portrayed a population dependent on fishing and the hunting of large mammals. Areas where relatively high concentrations of Upper Palaeolithic material have been recovered are the Doward, the meanders of the lower Wye and the Caldicot Levels. Consideration of the Doward is included within this book as the finds tell us much about early life in Monmouthshire.

The Sites and Monuments Record (S.M.R.) for Gwent, whose borders were nearly co-terminous with those of Monmouthshire, lists only a handful of finds, located close to the courses of the major rivers. They have usually been discovered by chance although, in the case of those at Usk, riverside development has played a role. Finds include a single flint core and a selection of blades, flakes and waste material. One can imagine the flint-knapper manufacturing and shaping tools for those fishing from the nearby banks. There is a small concentration of finds a few kilometres west of the town of Caldicot. Of these, by far the most important include a *Levallois* flake (ST 49 86), a Palaeolithic tool named after a site at *Levallois-perret* in Paris, two handaxes (ST 49 86) and a series of associated flake and waste material. Although the distribution of finds is mainly concentrated within the east and north of the county, there is a single find, a *petit tranchet* axe, or transverse arrowhead, of Mesolithic date, from close to the village of Michaelstone-y-Fedw (ST 23 83), near Cardiff, and approximately 0.5km west of the Afon Rhymni. To the north-east of the county there are the spectacular King Arthur's Cave (SO 546 156) and Merlin's Cave (SO 556 153) along the Doward, in Herefordshire. More research is required between the Doward and the mouth of the Bristol Channel in order to reveal the pattern of hunter-gatherer activity in the area. St Peter's Cave (ST 539 927), just south of Chepstow, together with those on the Doward indicate that the Wye is the only focus for early prehistoric activity—very little from this period has been found to either the east or west of the river. Mesolithic and Palaeolithic hunter-gatherers looking for new territories and new hunting grounds would have used the rivers Severn and Wye to establish a foothold inland. Using boats and canoes they would have explored the rivers and their tributaries seeking temporary settlement sites.

Although the Doward has definite evidence of settlement, the Monmouthshire bank of the Wye opposite has produced only a few single 'stray' flint artefacts. The latter finds, mainly flint blades and waste flakes, may have either been lost during hunting expeditions or have derived from nearby settlement or occupation sites as yet undiscovered.

The Doward was formed by glacial activity followed by continuous erosion of the River Wye. The caves and rock shelters are situated in a large limestone outcrop overlooking the Wye between Symond's Yat and the village of Goodrich. Nearly all the evidence is located either close to or in the caves and rock shelters. King Arthur's Cave and Merlin's Cave have yielded an almost complete stratigraphic (layered) sequence spanning at least 15,000 years. The majority of artefacts from both sites, mainly flint and bone, have been lodged with Monmouth and Hereford museums.

Due to the good preservation qualities of the cave earth soils, the sequence at Merlin's Cave includes animal bone, bone tools, a human burial, shells, as well as flint and stone artefacts. Many of the animal bones excavated from the so-called 'mammoth' layer at King Arthur's Cave date from the last Ice Age between 10,000 and 30,000 years ago.

The animal remains from the 'mammoth' layer suggest a landscape totally devoid of trees, a landscape that was gripped by permafrost, not dissimilar to that of present day southern Greenland. The remains include those of woolly rhinoceros, horse, giant deer, wild ox, hyena and mammoth. During the height of the last glacial period (c.20,000 BC), it has been suggested the environment was far too cold for humans. Recent radiocarbon dating carried out on human bone from Paviland Cave, on the Gower coast in South Wales, suggests that the cave was inhabited around 26,550 BC—this new date replacing an old radiocarbon date of 16,510 BC. No other human remains between then and c.17,000 BC have been recovered from this part of Britain. So, for approximately ten thousand years, from 27,000 BC, most of Britain and all of Northern Europe lay in the grip of a severe ice age, beneath ice sheets that, in many areas, were at least 400m thick. The landscape of southern Britain was essentially a polar desert and almost totally uninhabitable. At the maximum limit, the ice sheets covered all of Wales, most of the west and north Midlands, and even engulfed the Wash and what is now the North Sea. The edge of the Welsh Ice Cap cut Monmouthshire in half (running north/south), and would have towered over present day Newport.

However, the final retreat of the ice sheets after 16,000 BC was very rapid. Afterwards, pollen evidence suggests that southern Britain was colonised by sub-arctic tundra plants including sedges, grasses, mosses, lichens and dwarf birch and willow. This rich mosaic of plant life encouraged migratory animals such as elk, horse and reindeer. On the tracks of these animals came small hunting communities, probably made up of immediate family groups. The cave systems along the Doward were possibly used as temporary summer encampments, for the semi-Arctic conditions around 12,000 BC would still have made the winter months somewhat inhospitable, with average temperatures perhaps as low as -5 degrees centigrade.

Apart from a short and very severe 'blip' between 11,000 and 10,000 BC (the Loch Lomond stadial or cold phase), the climate gradually warmed, encouraging a completely new set of plants and animals. Birch, willow, juniper and, in some areas, pine were succeeded in their northward migration by elm, lime and alder.

From the onset of the Mesolithic (Middle Stone Age, from 10,000-4,000 BC), oak, hazel and elm followed, and flourished during the so-called 'climatic optimum' around 7,500 BC, when average summer temperatures were at least one or two degrees higher than today. Very little in the way of economic or social change is apparent at the transition from the Upper Palaeolithic to the Early Mesolithic, a transition now believed to have been more subtle than was once thought.

The archaeological concept of transition is traditionally linked to environmental and climatic change. What tends to be ignored is the change in ideology and the adaptation to new surroundings and resources. The gradual transition from the Upper Palaeolithic to the Early Mesolithic would have lasted well over 3,000 years and dates, therefore, tend to be rather arbitrary. A few artefacts indicate this change at King Arthur's Cave. Flint tools tend to become smaller and more specialised, suggesting modification of hunting strategy to cope with the new range of animals. In addition, microlithic (small stone) blades which would have been inserted into wooden arrow shafts, have been found in many of the caves and rock shelters along the Doward.

Advanced hunter-gatherers: The Mesolithic in Monmouthshire
Early excavations at King Arthur's Cave and Merlin's Cave have revealed a limited number of Mesolithic bone and flint tools, shells, animal bones and human remains. Recent work in 1993 in a series of caves and rock shelters above the Seven Sisters rock stack, have confirmed the theory that continuous occupation occurred in this area for well over 15,000 years, from the Upper Palaeolithic through to the Bronze Age and beyond.

From one rock shelter, Madoc's Shelter (approximately 250 metres south of King Arthur's Cave), a number of pierced cowrie shells were discovered. Mesolithic in date, and imported from the west coast of Britain, the shells probably formed part of a necklace. This and many other artefacts recovered from cave sites within the locality suggest a well-organised and economically advanced community.

Gradual changes in climate and environment were complemented by changes in technology, ideas and population. The environmental

Seven Sisters rock stacks overlooking the Wye valley. Above these are a line of caves and rock shelters, including Arthur's Cave and Madoc's rock shelter

record suggests that colonisation by broad-leaved woodland (also known as 'wildwood' or 'climax' woodland) was progressing rapidly from the south. Within this woodland, one could imagine people from temporary encampments gathering seasonal fruits, seeds and berries, while hunting parties stalked the new animals such as red deer, roe deer and wild pig.

The rising temperatures had a dramatic effect on sea level. Over a period of about 3,000 years, the sea level rose well over thirty metres, as ice which had accumulated on land melted and fed the oceans (Simmons & Tooley, 1981). The plain, which had once extended from South Wales to Somerset and been populated by mammals such as red deer and aurochs, (a large and wild form of cattle), was gradually eroded as the Bristol Channel was formed. By about 6,500 BC Britain became an island.

Within Monmouthshire, nearly all Mesolithic activity is confined to the major river tributaries and shores of the newly formed Bristol Channel. This suggests that the Severn Estuary, still increasing in size, and the smaller river tributaries leading off it, were the first areas to be colonised. Here, fish, small game and nuts, fruits and berries abounded. Nevertheless, a few small Late Mesolithic flint scatters have been recorded around the towns of Abergavenny and Usk. Conversations with Frank Olding, curator of Abergavenny Museum, suggest that sites further north within the upland zone are more numerous than was once thought. Savory (1961) has suggested that finds such as mace-heads, which have been found on these upland sites, may date from the Mesolithic. Scatters were probably the result of seasonal hunting parties, travelling in an area covered in light birch and pine woodland. The majority of sites are Late Mesolithic (6,500-3,500 BC) and one can assume that migration and eventual settlement of northern Monmouthshire and eventually southern Herefordshire came from the south, with groups moving up the Severn, Wye and Usk valleys.

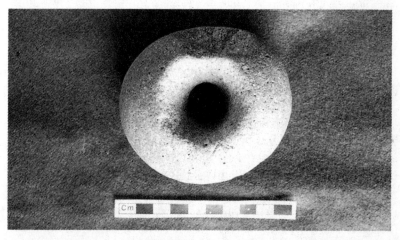

Mace-head made from a pebble found in a stream near to Little Berth-Glyd Farm, Llantilio Crossenny

Monmouthshire's Late Mesolithic communities took full advantage of all the available food resources. Across the Bristol Channel at Westward Ho! there is evidence (mainly from from coastal middens—refuse dumps consisting of marine shells) for the seasonal harvesting of hazelnuts, molluscs and fish. The evidence suggests that a greater emphasis was placed on gathering and fishing than on hunting, although the hunting communities on

7

either side of the Bristol Channel would have been spoiled for choice. The lower latitudes would have supported oak, lime, hazel and alder—mixed deciduous woodland (Huntley, 1990). Initially, the forest floor was cleared so as to attract large forest foraging animals such as deer and aurochs. Small patches of forest were cut back using flint knives and axes. The floor was burned to encourage re-growth which in turn would encourage grazing animals and thus much needed food for an ever-increasing human population. Later, during the Neolithic period (3,500-2,000 BC), woodland was also cleared for small allotment-style gardens. These plots became much larger as the demand for prime agricultural land increased. The abundance of food resources, a warmer climate and improved hunting technology would have led to an increase in the population of each group and intensification of interaction and alliances with neighbouring groups. As one progresses through the Mesolithic, important shifts occur within society. Temporary encampments and the associated moving around the landscape, hunting, gathering and foraging for seasonal resources, started to give way to more permanent bases. This change, possibly more than any other, provided the incentive to adopt agriculture during the Neolithic, though this change, as with the others, was gradual and not clearly defined.

It is most likely that settlement in Monmouthshire resulted from the consolidation of this prime hunting and gathering territory. This consolidation may have been due to an over-spill of population from adjoining areas, especially as the Severn Estuary increased in size. But why settle in this area?

The increase in population, although leading to greater social and political complexity, would eventually have placed an immense strain on the existing resources. The resulting demand for more land in which to hunt, gather and forage in order to sustain this increasing population may have created political instability between neighbouring communities. As a consequence, recognized territories may have been established which themselves helped create a more permanent society.

When one talks of neighbours one imagines a relationship that draws upon communal identity, an identity that relies upon social and political contact in the form of exchange or trade, and common ideology as well as (in most cases) a mutual understanding of territory. Usually, these components ensure a peaceful co-existence or, at least, a tolerance between neighbours. The need to secure social and political alliances with neighbouring communities would be of paramount importance in the process of territory formation. It is these constraints that may have forced breakaway kinship groups from over-populated areas to migrate away from their established ancestral homelands and beyond the territories of their neighbours. That is probably how the first groups arrived in Monmouthshire, where the process would eventually have repeated itself as further groups headed north. Within the hinterlands and coastal levels of Monmouthshire, the availability of seasonal fruits, nuts and seeds from rich, lush woodland, plus fish from the numerous streams and rivers, would have limited the need for hunting, and perhaps encouraged the uptake of more formal agriculture.

A comparison with recent hunter-gatherer societies

As we have seen, the evidence is limited to only the few artefacts (such as flint or stone) that have withstood the rigours of time. To build a better and more cohesive picture, other ideas and methods have to be introduced. Ethnography, for example, enables us to develop analogies between past and present cultures. Many hunting ideas, strategies and traditions characteristic of present-day hunter-gatherer societies, such as the San Bush people of the Kalahari or the Eskimos of the frozen Arctic wastes, may be applied to hunter-gatherers from remote prehistory.

The traditional concept that animals were merely caught, killed and eaten during the Mesolithic, and, indeed, the Palaeolithic is at best simplistic, at worst wholly misleading. Hunting plays a minor role in the day-to-day activities of the !Kung (San) bush people of the Kalahari in Namibia (Lee, 1968). Around 70% of their diet consists of vegetable foods, with the remaining 30% largely made up of small invertebrate animals such as grubs and larvae, both of which are very high in protein. The hunting of large animals is usually conducted on an occasional basis. Similarly, forest gatherers like the Baka people (pygmies) of central Cameroon rely heavily on gathered food, where the consumption of meat has a more symbolic role. Their 'big game', (in this case, small forest monkeys), are hunted on a ritual basis, similar to that evidenced by the Australian Aborigines. In both societies everything in nature is considered sacred. Great sorrow is expressed when an animal is hunted and killed, for animals are not just a source of food, they are a symbolic component of daily life.

One can imagine, in Mesolithic society, that when an animal was killed and prepared, ritual chanting and dancing may have taken place prior to eating; the dancing may have involved the re-enactment of the hunt and final kill. Cave art from Trois Freres in France depicts a dancing human—perhaps a sorcerer—wearing antler head gear, whilst at the Mesolithic lowland dwelling site of Star Carr in Yorkshire, complete sets of red deer antler, which may have formed part of ceremonial masks, were recovered.

Apart from symbolic and ritual use, meat may also have possessed political significance during the Mesolithic. The equal sharing of meat in many contemporary hunter-gatherer societies dispels any notion of hierarchy or economic status; the hunting group becomes one. In !Kung society, possession of an animal killed in the hunt is not regarded as ownership—the arrows used are usually made by other individuals within the hunting party and loaned to the hunter, so reducing any legitimate right of direct ownership of the dead animal. The meat belongs to the group and its distribution allows everyone to participate.

The Mesolithic *petit tranchet* axe mentioned earlier and found near Michaelstone-y-Fedw may have been accidentally lost by a hunting party venturing inland through dense deciduous oak and hazel woodland, their dug-out canoes securely attached to the nearby shores.

The Neolithic

The Neolithic (New Stone Age) is the latest of the three 'stone ages', and represents the introduction of agriculture to Britain. It is now thought that this revolution began about ten thousand years ago in the 'fertile crescent'—present day Lebanon, Israel and Syria. By about 4,000 BC, there is evidence that small 'garden' style allotments existed throughout the fertile valleys of western Europe, although many parts of Britain would still have been covered by dense forest. At the beginning of the Neolithic, around 3,700 BC, the pollen evidence for Monmouthshire, indeed Britain, suggests a clearance programme was under way. There is a clear decline in elm and lime, possibly due to the outbreak of a fungus akin to Dutch Elm disease which led to the clearance, or possibly simply a result of clearance itself. Along with this decline, the pollen evidence highlights a rise in weeds associated with cultivation such as plantains. It seems that by this time domesticated sheep, continental cattle, pigs and seed corn had also been imported into Britain. But the introduction of agriculture was no 'overnight affair'. During the preceding Mesolithic (10,000 - 4,000 BC), there is evidence for the controlled herding and corralling of wild animals, in addition to the seasonal harvesting of wild fruits, roots and nuts. The rigid divide often expressed between a hunting and gathering way of life and a farming economy is in many ways misleading. Rather, the evidence suggests a gradual process of economic and social change.

Perhaps surprisingly, it is not the economic and settlement evidence that has survived the rigours of time, but monuments commemorating the dead. Elaborate chambered tombs made of large stones, or megaliths, dominate the Neolithic landscape of Monmouthshire and elsewhere. Originally, these monuments would have been covered by an earth mound, leaving the entrance or fore-court area and the passage as the only visible part. In common with present day religious buildings, areas of the tomb would have been restricted to particular social strata within the community. But archaeological evidence suggests that these tombs were more than just repositories for the dead, for the Neolithic tombs of Monmouthshire appear to have had a social and political as well as a symbolic function.

Finds from the Neolithic are more numerous than those from earlier periods, though still do not amount to much. Many have been discovered during the preparation of the ground for building construction. At least five major find sites have been located in Newport, three in Cwmbran, one in Pontypool and two in Abergavenny. Sites are usually close to major river courses, where water was easily obtainable and fish available.

A number of other sites that have been discovered recently in the Black Mountains and the southern part of the Brecon Beacons are located well over 400m above sea level. One can interpret these

11

Decorated rim of Neolithic pottery from Abergavenny's
Flannel Street excavation (1965)

sites as hunter-gatherer grounds, lands or territories. During the Late Neolithic, the uplands may have been used as summer pastures for small, seasonal semi-nomadic groups. The lowlands and valleys to the south would have made ideal winter encampments. This type of pastoral farming is commonly used today in Alpine regions. One can only guess, however, whether similar animal husbandry was practiced in these upland areas.

There is also a sparse distribution of chambered monuments which includes four burial chambers: Heston Brake (ST 505 887), Y Gaer Llwyd (ST 448 967), Thornwell Farm (ST 539 917) and Gwern y Cleppa (ST 276 851). Interestingly, these monuments are located in the east of the county and away from the large Black Mountains group in southern Powys.

These tombs, and many throughout Wales, appear to follow a set of landscape rules. Firstly, they are never sited on the highest point within the immediate landscape. Secondly, they all appear either to be locally aligned to various topographic points, or follow a more regulated ideology in which the passage and chamber is aligned east-west. Reasons for this are unclear, although it may be linked to the sun's rising in the east, which may represent life, and setting in the west, symbolizing death. Burials continued on an east-west alignment even with the advent of Christianity. In the case of the Thornwell tomb, Heston Brake and Gwern y Cleppa, the monuments all look over the northern extent of the Severn Estuary/

Bristol Channel, similar to how the eighteen or so tombs around the fertile valleys of the Black Mountains all have views towards those mountains.

The recent excavation of a Neolithic mound and Bronze Age burials at Thornwell Farm near Chepstow also highlights the continual use of sites through time. The idea of continuity is further reinforced by an examination of the distribution of Neolithic and Bronze Age find spots—all are close together. Also close to many Neolithic scatters are a few isolated scatters of earlier Mesolithic material. This chronological distribution reinforces the notion that prehistoric sites were in continuous use over many thousands of years, probably the result of many generations of familiarity with the landscape—a social, economic and symbolic knowledge that created a sense of belonging to and an identity with an area. Associated with this would have been the gradual change from hunting, fishing and gathering to short-term and eventually long term commitment to agriculture and animal domestication.

Archaeologists have previously considered that change between the Mesolithic and the Neolithic was due to invading peoples. Stanford (1991), suggests that 'the descendants of these hunters ... may have become guides, porters and perhaps stockmen for subsequent Neolithic people'. If this were the case, where did these Neolithic people come from? It is clear that the construction of tomb monuments throughout Britain occurred around the same time and the invasion theory, therefore, seems highly improbable, unless it was of ideas instead of people, just as 'Americanisation' can be seen as an 'invasion' of our way of life.

It would appear that only hunting parties and not Neolithic settlers were interested in venturing into the north-western part of Monmouthshire—the Brecon Beacons and the area close to present day Tredegar and Ebbw Vale. Here, 500m above sea level, the landscape would have been bare and inhospitable. The mountains may have also been considered taboo and dangerous. We have suggested previously (Children & Nash, 1994, 20-22) that settlement and monument building in west Herefordshire was only acceptable on the west-facing slopes of the Golden Valley, approximately 18km east of the Black Mountains and in full sight of the mountains. Likewise, similar distribution exists around the upper

Wye and Usk valleys which appear to be facing the Black Mountains from the west, in particular large topographical features that are highly visible such as spurs, gullies, valleys and escarpments. In Monmouthshire, the finds around Gilwern, Abergavenny and, to the north-east, along the Afon Honddu appear to mark the limit of Neolithic activity around the mountains. Here Neolithic communities would have thrived, we have suggested, but were bound by religious taboo from venturing further towards the mountains. Quite the reverse occurs during the Bronze Age when round barrows and cairns were sited on hill and mountain tops. This change in burial monument location is probably due to a change in symbolic and ritual ideology. Perhaps our Bronze age ancestors wished to be closer to their god(s)!

However, the four chambered monuments of Monmouthshire are not in the uplands, but are sited on the lower undulating hinterland, close to the Gwent Levels and the Bristol Channel beyond. A few kilometres east, beyond the county boundary, is a possible long chambered tomb on Garway Hill (SO 441 252) in Herefordshire. As well as being located close to the tomb at Y Gaer Llywd, the site suggests that it was probably part of the Monmouthshire (South Wales) Group and not part of the Black Mountains group.

The tombs all appear to be of different style, though they all possess a chamber built from a single capstone which is supported by a series of uprights and were originally covered by a mound. They have yielded limited Neolithic finds, which include flint and polished stone axes, flint tools and associated waste material. Many have argued that the Monmouthshire monuments may form part of an ideological and symbolic chain between the monuments of the Severn-Cotswold region, the Gower coast and west Wales. However, our opinion is that each marks an independent political territory which often joined with similar neighbouring territories for large undertakings, such as the building of monuments.

The construction of chambered tombs, with the deposit of individuals' possessions (known as grave goods), show that they were a religious people who believed in an afterlife. Unfortunately, there has been little recent excavation of the Monmouthshire monuments and, therefore, very little in the way of bone, pottery and flint has been collected from them, except for Thornwell which was excavated in 1990-91. The same problem applies to nearly all tombs throughout Wales, though at Ty Isaf, a long chambered tomb near Talgarth in Powys, crushed bones of at least twenty individuals, together with Neolithic pottery, a polished stone axe and a collection of flint arrowheads were discovered. Similar ways of burying the dead are practised all over the world today. Even in Victorian Britain, the dead were sometimes interred with small items of jewellry and prepared and dressed for the journey to the after-life. Similar practices would have taken place at Y Gaer Llwyd, Gwern y Cleppa, Heston Brake and Thornwell.

Trying to understanding the living is more difficult. Very little organic material such as arrow shafts, buckets and canoes, animal products like skins, tooth pendants, bone mattock handles, and food remains have survived.

Apart from the more obvious structures, the county also boasts a number of standing stones which are possibly Late Neolithic or Early Bronze Age in origin. In addition, substantial quantities of flints have been recovered mainly as a result of town development, particularly around the outer suburbs of Newport overlooking the rivers Usk and Ebbw. Further to the east and also within the centre of Abergavenny, excavations have revealed Late Neolithic and Early Bronze Age material including decorated pottery and flint. These scatters, usually containing only a few flint tools and waste material are virtually the only evidence for actual settlements in the Neolithic period in Monmouthshire.

The Production and Use of Prestige Artefacts
From the south and east of the county are a series of single 'prestige' finds that indicate possible trading alliances or seasonal expeditions outside Monmouthshire. These prestige goods, twelve in total, consist of polished stone and flint axes. Why prestige? It has been shown that if used, most polished stone axes would shatter. However, by shaping and polishing an axe, an article is created which, although functional in theory, in fact symbolises power and prestige and, above all, a stratified society. An assumption can be made, therefore, that both flint and polished stone axes were status symbols owned and controlled by the most powerful. The origins of such prestige items indicates some form of trade with areas as far

away as Cornwall, Cumbria and Scandinavia. At least two examples from southern Sweden are known within or near the county; a Scandinavian flat-butted axe was found in Benchwood, an eastern suburb of Newport (SO 33 88), whilst an identically shaped axe was also found within the root system of an old yew tree on the Great Doward, just across the border in Herefordshire. An axe from the Scafell Pike axe factory in Cumbria was found on English Newton Common (SO 52 15), whilst two fine examples of Greenstone axes from the Penzance area were discovered close to the M4, north-west of Newport (SO 30 88). A further three axes (SO 29 86) were discovered in Newport as a result of housing development. A polished stone and a polished flint axe were also found north of Abergavenny, at the foot of the Black Mountains.

Polished Neolithic stone axe found in the garden of Glebe Cottage, Llantilio Pertholey

Were these axes shaped at the source areas or were they carved near the find spots from imported stone? There is evidence of extensive flint waste material around Great Langdale in Cumbria, suggesting that at least rough axes were made at source, even if they were re-worked on reaching their destination. An alternative has been suggested (Briggs, 1973, 318-320) that, at least during the early Neolithic, the material used for creating stone axes may have originated from glacial erratics from Cumbria, North Wales and the Pennines that were transported and deposited by ice during the last glacial advance some 18,000 years ago. However, this theory does

Polished Neolithic flint axe found after ploughing at
Chapel Farm, Clytha

not account for flint from Wiltshire and stone from Cornwall, areas both lying to the south of the ice margin. The only way of importing this material into the county would have been through trade with other groups, or as a result of expeditions. In addition, we would suggest that in order to add prestige to one of these axes, the flint or stone used to make the axe must have come direct from the source area, though in the case of the Swedish axes, trading was most probably the method of acquisition. By employing valuable time for axe expeditions, a restricted and exclusive product was created. Cheap imitations would not have been good enough! The use, therefore, of glacial erratics to make prestige items would have been pointless, especially when glacial deposits are so abundant on the valley floors and the intermediate slopes of Monmouthshire. Developing this theme further, it is likely that the organisation of trade expeditions during the Middle and Late Neolithic would have been socially and politically complex, adding to the resultant perceived prestige. This organisation could not have been undertaken by small scale agricultural groups, it would quite possibly have involved an alliance between a number of groups bound together by kinship and/or a common ancestry, each with its area of territory.

Non-polished artefacts may also have been prestige items. A perforated axe hammer, the provenance of which is unknown, originates from an axe factory at Cwm Mawr, Cromdon Hill,

Montgomeryshire (Shotton, 1961). Other examples have also been found at Cwmdu and St Julian's Wood, Newport. Similarly, a single mace-head found in a stream close to Little Berth-Glyd Farm, Llantilio Crossenny, has been fashioned from a large pebble, possibly from the coast. This mace-head may have had a number of uses, either as a weight for a digging stick or as a weapon (Grimes, 1951).

Uskmouth & Magor Pill

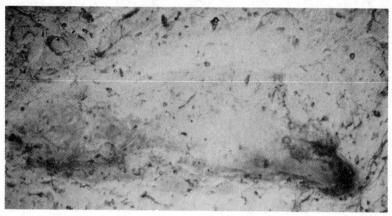

© GGAT

One of the prints of a left foot, showing the indentation of the big toe to the bottom right

> Nothing to be seen
> Location: Severn Estuary, to the east of the
> mouth of the Usk (SO 34 82 & SO 44 83)

In Monmouthshire, and elsewhere, evidence for the Mesolithic is to say the least, limited. The physical remains usually consist of a few pieces of waste flint and the occasional tool. However, from the intertidal foreshore of the Gwent Levels at Uskmouth and Magor Pill, two sets of footprints consisting of 45 impressions dating from the Late Mesolithic (3720+/-80 BC & 4250+/-80 BC respectively) were discovered. Dates for both sites were taken from the overlying peat. The footprints from both sites were imprinted into fine estuarine clays. Then, over the millennia they became fossilised underneath peat and successive transgressions and regressions of the Bristol Channel.

Judging by the direction of the footprints, heading to the southeast, they may well have been those of a small fishing party and it may be that fishing and gathering territories were gradually being established. Though the only evidence we have is from the foot-

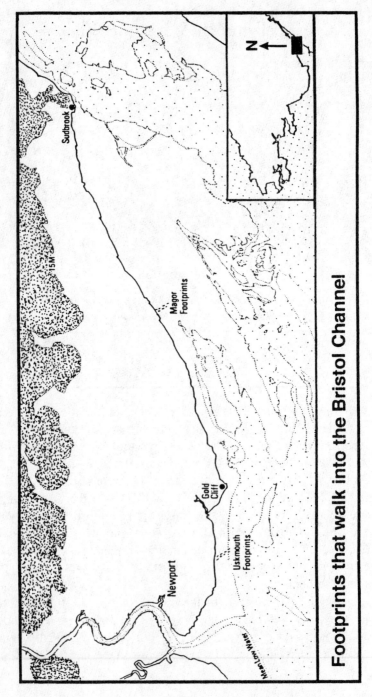

Footprints that walk into the Bristol Channel

prints, their chance discovery suggests that activity in and around the Gwent Levels during this period was high.

During the Late Mesolithic, the estuary would have had a similar shore-line to that of today. Within the complete sequence (4.5m) where the footprints were found were three separate peat layers, which suggests that the climate on three occasions was wet enough for the formation of reed beds. The excavation revealed a history of sea-level rise and fall with the deposition of clays, muds and silts. The full sequence dates from about 7,000 BC and is comparable with other sequences throughout Britain.

The Uskmouth footprints were laid down in three trails—made by three people. Two trails run in parallel for about 25 metres and lie 10 metres apart. Both sets of footprints belonged to males. The footprints from the third trail were smaller and may have been those of a child, possibly accompanying his or her father on a fishing expedition. It was possible to determine the size of the feet, and hence their owners' stature, along with the number of steps per minute and thus speed at which they travelled. The adult males would have been about 1.7m tall, and it appears the child of about 1.35m height was keeping up with one and outpacing the other! One adult and the child are thought to have been walking at just under 5km an hour, the other adult dawdling at just under 4km an hour. It has to be said that these calculations are subject to a fairly wide tolerance of error of plus or minus 15%.

Some 370 metres east-south-east of the footprints, a perforated antler mattock was discovered on exposed estuarine clays, at the same level as the footprints. Mattocks (and any other Mesolithic tools) in Wales are extremely rare. This antler mattock may have been used for clearing away brushwood, or perhaps for raking through the mud and silt in order to search for shellfish. A similar mattock from Splash Point, Rhyl was radiocarbon dated to 4560+/-80 BC, in the Late Mesolithic.

In 1990, at Magor Pill, 11km north-east and up the coast from Uskmouth, a set of 14 footprints was discovered. They were located some 90m south of the present shore-line, beyond the high water mark and 50m away from the coastal saltmarsh. This set of prints—a single trail set in clay—was overlain by peat which was radio-carbon dated to 3720+/-80 BC (a similar date to the Uskmouth peat sequence). The prints, believed to be those of a barefoot man, were much larger than those at Uskmouth. It has been calculated that the man would have taken a size 12 shoe, if such were available, and have been just under 2m tall. Along with these, were the possible footprints of another child.

King Arthur's Cave

Cave showing occupation from the Upper Palaeolithic through to
the Bronze Age and beyond
Location: 8km from Monmouth, 13km from Ross (SO 546 156)
Access: Via a public footpath from a public car park
Forestry Commission rules and regulations apply
when visiting this site

This cave can be approached from either Monmouth or Ross-on-Wye via the A40. Take the turning, 4km from Monmouth, sign-posted 'Doward'. Follow the road across the A40 to Ganarew and turn left at the T junction—the road now running parallel to the A40. After 600m take the first right, again signposted 'Doward' (and 'Heritage Centre'). Proceed along this extremely narrow and winding road for about 2km and turn right onto a rough forest track. Approximately 200m from this turning is a small car park. From the car park, walk back towards the track turning. There is a small footpath on the left. Carefully walk down this path, past a disused quarry and a series of rock overhangs. The footpath continues past three large rock shelters (at least one of these rock shelters may be mistaken for King Arthur's Cave). Follow the footpath for 250m and King Arthur's Cave is located at the end of this rock outcrop. In front of the cave is a large earthen ridge—the spoil heap from the 1927 excavation. The cave itself is recognised by a large double entrance.

King Arthur's Cave was extensively excavated in 1870/71, 1926/27 and 1954/55. Prior to this, the cave was used for iron ore extraction during the eighteenth and nineteenth centuries which destroyed most of the archaeological evidence. However, the 1870/71 excavations revealed that the sediment stratigraphy around the cave walls and the central column that divides the two cave sections (close to the entrance) was virtually undisturbed. The material recovered from this section revealed finds that span the period from the Early Upper Palaeolithic (latter part of the Old Stone Age) to the Bronze Age (c.2,000 BC), a total of some 50,000 years.

The five distinct stratified layers represent a series of cold (glacial) and warm (interglacial) episodes. The upper cave surface (most recent) consists of a stalactite floor. Associated with this layer were the remains of badger, birds and fox. Also present were a small number of pottery sherds, probably of Bronze Age date.

The second layer consists of an upper cave earth, 0.6m thick. Intermixed with this layer were the bones of horse, cave bear and beaver as well as flint material dating back to the Upper Palaeolithic. Below this, a third layer, approximately one metre deep revealed evidence of possible glacial activity (suggesting that the ice margin was close by). The presence of red sand and, more

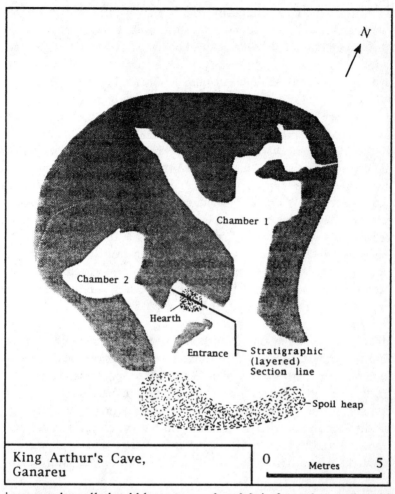

| King Arthur's Cave, Ganareu | 0 | Metres | 5 |

importantly, rolled pebbles suggest that debris from the nearby old red sandstone outcrops on Coppet Hill and Huntsham Hill had been transported west, down the Wye Valley, past King Arthur's Cave. Alternatively, this layer may have been formed by the water seepage which carried debris through fissures from the surrounding porous rocks. The fourth layer, a late glacial deposit, consisted of hearth material (charcoal and ash) incorporating remains of giant elk, horse and ox, as well as further Upper Palaeolithic flints including scrapers and blades. The fifth layer, approximately 6 metres down and aptly named the 'mammoth' layer, was formed by a lower and more ancient cave-earth. In amongst this layer were the remains of mammoth, elk, reindeer and woolly rhinoceros. Some of the bones had possibly been gnawed by hyenas, meaning that at one point in the cave's early history it might have been inhabited by hyenas, cave bears and other mammals. This being the case, Upper Palaeolithic hunter-gatherers would have certainly used this cave on a temporary basis rather than on a permanent one! Also present were large quantities of flint dated to the Upper Palaeolithic.

The 1926/7 excavations directed by Herbert Taylor provided a more detailed report on the available stratigraphy. Six layers were discovered: three Upper Palaeolithic, one Mesolithic, one Neolithic and a recently formed 'stalactite' floor. Although correlating closely with the sequences uncovered by Symonds some fifty years before, they were better defined and above all, intact. In total, 720 pieces of flint were recovered as well as numerous pieces of bone. Indeed, even the spoil heap from the 1870/71 excavation was excavated! Here, many artefacts were recovered including a possible *tranchet* axe, flint scrapers, burins (awls) and large quantities of flint flake and waste material.

The origin of the flint is difficult to establish. No fine quality flint is known locally, therefore it would appear that it was imported, probably from South Wales. If so, either long distance trade with other groups or long distance expeditions to areas containing flint would have been necessary. Judging by the quantity of flint recovered, that incidentally spans the Upper Palaeolithic right through to the Bronze Age, the exchange and/or expedition networks would have been well established, using the local waterways and ancient tracks.

Also recovered were a number of bone and antler artefacts. Many of these were used for digging and chopping. However, one particular piece, a bone rod, was decorated with a possible 'stylised' fish design. Although now considered to be of questionable origin, this design is nevertheless similar to Mesolithic 'portable' decorated artefacts from southern Scandinavia.

Herbert Taylor's excavation uncovered two hearths, both crammed full with valuable bone deposits. The first hearth had been used and reused over many thousands of years and contained bones of ox, deer, pig, horse, beaver, brown bear and hedgehog. Also present were many tools including 'imported' pebbles. These were used as either hammerstones or polishing/rubbing stones for the production of tools. Other pebbles were present in many colours, though particularly red and green. Their function is unknown, but it has been suggested that they were decorative.

Below the first hearth was a thin yellow soil layer. This too, revealed both flint and bone evidence. Obviously older than the first hearth, this layer revealed yet more evidence of animals, including now extinct giant deer, together with ox, wild horse, hare, pika, lemming and hedgehog.

The second hearth, 0.3m thick, was again very rich in bone material. Present were giant deer, horse, ox and pika. Some of the bone had been split longitudinally in order for the then cave dwellers to extract valuable protein enriched marrow. Along with the bone material were large amounts of burnt flint including scrapers, points and blades. All the flint material from both hearths is very similar in form to that from other Upper Palaeolithic cave sites on the Gower Coast and in the Mendip Hills.

So, one can imagine these hearths being a focal point for our ancestral hunter-gatherers and where the day's catch, probably a deer or wild horse, was cooked at night. Stories which had been passed down from generation to generation were told as they devoured the succulent meal. Possibly, meat and flint were 'offered' to the fire as a way of thanking the deities for providing a good kill.

Whilst there were no results published of the 1954/55 excavation, a recent survey in the Doward area in 1993 has confirmed that the prehistory of this cave and other neighbouring caves and rock shelters is indeed complex. The continuous human presence, especially during the late Upper Palaeolithic and early Mesolithic (10,000-8,000 BC), is a vital key to the colonisation and subsequent settlement of Monmouthshire and Herefordshire.

Merlin's Cave

Cave showing occupation from the Upper Palaeolithic
through to the Bronze Age and beyond
Location: 13km from Ross, 8km from Monmouth (SO 556 153)
Access: Via a public footpath from a public car park
Forestry Commission rules and regulations apply
when visiting this site

From the car park above King Arthur's Cave (for directions to this car park please refer to the entry for King Arthur's Cave), proceed for 1.5km along a forestry track towards The Biblins (a youth adventure centre). From The Biblins, turn left onto a track that follows the course of the River Wye. The track soon becomes a narrow footpath which you follow for 400m. Directly left is a steep incline. The entrance to Merlin's Cave is in two sections: a lower chamber and an alcove. Together, they can be clearly seen approximately 60m up the slope (the entrance resembles the 'eye sockets' of a human skull). Extreme caution should be observed when climbing up to this cave.

South facing, Merlin's Cave is located on an enormous rock outcrop, one of many with numerous caves and rock shelters that encompass the whole of the Doward meander; from the jutting rock stacks of the Seven Sisters to Symonds Yat. The caves were formed by water seeping and eroding through carboniferous limestone rock fissures.

Merlin's Cave, like King Arthur's Cave, was thoroughly excavated in the late 1920s by T.F. Hewer of the University of Bristol Spelaeological Society, who also gave it its name. Sadly, both Merlin's and Arthur's Caves were exploited for iron ore during the eighteenth and nineteenth centuries which has damaged the archaeological evidence for earlier times. Indeed, there is evidence of much earlier iron ore extraction at both caves during the Roman period. Despite this, however, both caves have evidence of a human presence throughout prehistory; certainly as far back as the Late Upper Palaeolithic (15-10,000 BC), though at Merlin's Cave, very little Upper Palaeolithic material has been recovered. Only a handful of flint artefacts have been found of which a schoolboy's find, a Bronze Age razor, is the most notable. At the back of the cave, Hewer's team uncovered the remains of a possible burial, although it was difficult to date. Numerous bone artefacts were also recovered including a bone point (sheep), a perforated tooth (dog or fox) and two bone spatulas. Also found were two perforated amber beads and small chippings of chert which were either Mesolithic or Upper Palaeolithic in date. Pottery was also present—a small collection of Bronze Age Beaker and Roman black burnished pottery sherds. Finally, a fourth century Roman coin was found, dating from the period of Constantine the Great, AD 330-335.

Within the cave earths was a large collection of bone material which had been built up over many thousands of years. This gives a unique insight into past climatic and environmental change. These

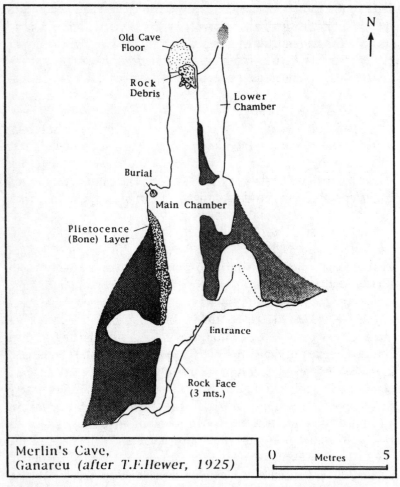

N

Old Cave Floor

Rock Debris

Lower Chamber

Burial

Main Chamber

Plietocence (Bone) Layer

Entrance

Rock Face (3 mts.)

Merlin's Cave, Ganareu *(after T.F.Hewer, 1925)*

0   Metres   5

bones, along with water action, cave earths, limestone and rock debris, have created a conglomerate platform located against the left wall, near the cave entrance. It is approximately 4.5m long and at least 1.4m thick. Previous investigations have revealed that cave inhabitants included common lemming, Arctic lemming, European beaver, bank vole, short-tailed vole, northern vole, field vole and numerous birds. The presence of some of these small mammals suggests that the climate was a good deal colder than today, possibly that of a tundra-scrub environment, devoid of trees.

Gwern y Cleppa

Chambered tomb with the stones visible
Location: 4km south-west of Newport (ST 276 850)
Access: On private land but can be seen from a nearby track

This monument is located approximately 40m north of the M4, to the west of Newport. From junction 28 on the M4 take the road signposted 'Cleppa Park Business Park', turning right again shortly afterwards into the business park. From the far end of the business park, walk northwards along a rough track to the motorway. Follow the track for approximately 200m, crossing the M4 via a bridge. Walk through the field to the left parallel with the M4. An old wall separates this field from the next. The Cleppa Park monument is visible from a path close to a north-south orientated wall, about 100m away on a small south-facing ridge.

Gwern y Cleppa is possibly the remains of a long chambered tomb of the Cotswold-Severn tradition for traces still survive of a long mound, approximately 40m in length. The stones are now much disturbed. It was reported in 1897 that three (siliceous grey) sandstone uprights, were *in situ* (Barber & Williams, 1989, 131). Following a recent visit to the site, the authors hold the view that two of these still remain in position. A fallen capstone lies within what was once a large chambered area. A fourth upright lies recumbent underneath the capstone. It has been suggested that this formed a simple terminal chamber (Corcoran, 1969, 20).

The monument would have had a view of the Bristol Channel approximately 4.8km away to the south, though this is now blocked by the M4. The landscape setting is similar to that of nearby Tinkinswood and St Lythans (Glamorgan), in slightly undulating country. However, there are extensive views of the hills to the north and west. The monument is positioned between these hills, the fertile flood plains of the lower Usk Valley to the east, and the alluvial flats to the south and the Severn Estuary beyond. Close by, to the north, east and south, between one and two kilometres away, is the River Ebbw which flows into the Usk. Today, the monument is surrounded by woodland to the north and south-west.

The authors believe Gwern y Cleppa once formed part of a ritual landscape that involved a nearby standing stone (of Bronze Age date). Other monuments, now long since destroyed, may have dominated the lower Usk Valley, establishing a series of territorial markers along the valley, similar to those located along the upper Wye and Usk valleys around the Black Mountains.

Y Gaer Llwyd

Chambered tomb with series of uprights and collapsed capstone
Location: 7km south-east of Usk (ST 447 967)
Access: Lies adjacent to a road

This monument lies close to a series of Early Bronze Age monuments to the south including two stone circles, a standing stone and a round barrow cemetery. From the small town of Usk head east along the A472. Just before the road merges with the A449 Newport to Monmouth road, turn left onto the B4235. Approximately 8km along this road is the small hamlet of Gaerllwyd. Just before this settlement, Y Gaer Llwyd is signposted and clearly visible in a field on the right.

This monument, also known as Gaerllwyd and Garnllwyd, is located within a small area of rough scrubland and bushes, close to a hedge. It is now much disturbed, and the outer cairn has been destroyed by the combination of road construction and stone robbing. Castleden, (1992, 386) however, argues whether or not a covering mound ever existed. The plan and form of the monument, in particular two transverse portal stones, suggest that it is linked to the Severn-Cotswold tradition—Houlder (1978, 139) suggests the

Irish Sea group of monuments. Corcoran (1969, 20) refers to this monument as a Portal Dolmen: a central burial chamber surrounded by a series of upright stones supporting a single capstone, which would have then been covered by a mound of earth or stones.

What remains are a series of uprights, three of which support a large, partly collapsed capstone (3.2 x 2.5m). Two of these demarcate an entrance or divide two parts of a chamber. Around the chamber area are a series of fallen uprights which possibly demarcate a now destroyed passage and entrance area. Castleden (1992, 386) has noted that several stones from this monument have been incorporated into nearby modern buildings.

Heston Brake

Chambered tomb covered in scrub
Location: 6km south-west of Chepstow (ST 505 886)
Access: Visible from nearby road

From the border town of Chepstow, take the A48 towards Newport.
After some 4.5km take a left turn signposted 'Portskewett'. Proceed

down this road for 2km. The Heston Brake monument is on a small rise (25m above sea level) between two wooded areas in an open field on the right, 20m from the road. The tomb is at present overgrown with wild scrub and bushes. Visible to the north-east are the towers of the first Severn Bridge.

Located only 1.8km from the banks of the Severn Estuary, Heston Brake would have had a direct view to the Cotswolds beyond. The setting is similar to that of nearby Tinkinswood and Maes y Felin—a low undulating landscape of open fields. The soils surrounding the monument are associated with the River Severn flood plain and, during the Neolithic, the land would have probably been utilised for crops.

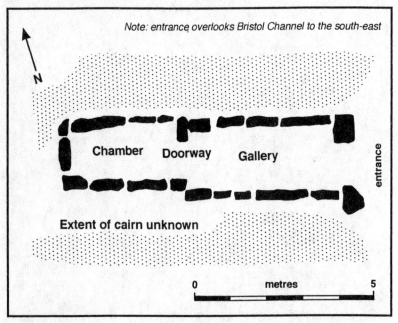

Heston Brake is a much disturbed site. The chamber and passage area is located within a long cairn aligned east-west and 22 metres long. The rectangular terminal chamber (3m x 1.4m), now without a capstone, lies at the eastern part of the mound. Consisting of nine uprights, the chamber plan lies off-line from the passage which merges into the chamber. Two uprights demarcate the transition point between the passage (4m in length) and the chamber

36

entrance—both of which are 1.5m wide. The merging of the two areas suggest that this monument may well be a gallery grave, in which the passage and burial chamber lack clear separation, and therefore be of middle to late Neolithic date. However, the architecture of the chamber and that of the passage are different which might suggest that the chamber is a later modification. An earlier chamber may therefore have existed. Houlder (1978) has suggested that Heston Brake, along with Y Gaer Llwyd, belongs to a western architectural style, rather than the nearby influences of the Severn-Cotswold tradition. Corcoran (1969, 45) argues that the plan is similar to the Ffostyll South chamber in the Black Mountains. Heston Brake was excavated during 1888 when the remains of human skeletons were found in the chamber area. However, it was noticed during the excavation that the mound had been opened on an earlier occasion.

Long Barrow and Round Barrow at Thornwell Farm

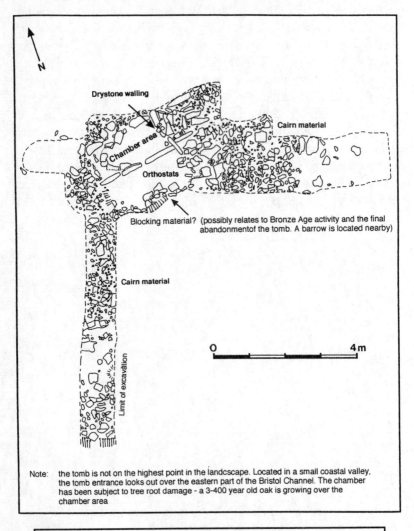

N

Drystone walling

Cairn material

Chamber area

Orthostats

Blocking material? (possibly relates to Bronze Age activity and the final abandonment of the tomb. A barrow is located nearby)

Cairn material

Limit of excavation

0   4 m

Note: the tomb is not on the highest point in the landscape. Located in a small coastal valley, the tomb entrance looks out over the eastern part of the Bristol Channel. The chamber has been subject to tree root damage - a 3-400 year old oak is growing over the chamber area

Long and round barrow
Location: 2.5km south of Chepstow (ST 539917)
Access: They are both adjacent to a road and housing estate

Approximately 2.5km south of the border town of Chepstow are two burial mounds—one Neolithic, the other Bronze Age. The Neolithic monument is one of the most exceptional discoveries made in recent years. Now located in the middle of a large housing estate, both monuments were unknown until 1990.

From the roundabout with the M48 south of Chepstow at the western end of the first Severn Bridge, take the road signposted to Thornwell. Proceed along this road for approximately 0.5km to a second roundabout. Take the third exit and follow the road around the hill. The old Thornwell Farm is on the right. The monument is clearly visible on the corner of Fountain Way, surrounded by low wooden fencing. What can be seen is a much disturbed mound, a large-butted capstone, kerbing and the remains of a chamber area.

The position in the landscape is similar to that of nearby Heston Brake. Both mounds have commanding views over the south-western extent of the Severn Estuary towards the Quantocks beyond, and are situated close to the confluence of the Wye and the Severn. The mound is positioned, not on the highest point, but on the intermediate slope of a small hillock. It overlooks not only the sea, but the immediate valley to the south.

It was described in an excavation report by the Glamorgan-Gwent Archaeological Trust who commented that the internal features of the mound had been much disturbed by tree root damage from a 300 year old oak.

Within the Neolithic mound were found the remains of four adults and two children, together with pottery dating from the Early Neolithic, and flint tools. The human bone appeared to have been both articulated and disarticulated; some of it was burnt. Also present was a large quantity of bones from birds of prey.

The presence of partially burnt disarticulated bones strengthens the suggestion that bodies may have been excarnated prior to 'burial'—where the bodies were laid out on platforms open to the elements. This was the practice of the Indians of the American north-west coast who, once the bones had been cleaned by carrion, would collect them and either burn and then store or directly store them in large urns, which would then be buried.

The mound, oval in shape, was delineated by a line of stone kerbing. Measuring approximately 16m x 10m, the tomb is most probably linked to the Severn-Cotswold tradition of burial monuments. One side of the chamber has a 'port-hole' upright which segregates the main chamber from the ante-chamber and entrance. During the tomb's use, the 'port-hole' would have restricted the visual access to the main chamber. Any ceremonial activity within the chamber could have only been witnessed by those interring the body or remains.

Close to the main chamber were also found two Early Bronze Age cist burials. The cists, rectangular in form, were constructed of stone slabs. In one cist were two adult males both lying in a crouching position, one on top of the other. Accompanying the burials was a barbed and tanged arrowhead and a corded-ware beaker pot dating from the same period as the burials.

The other mound close by has been classified as a Bronze Age round barrow, but has not been investigated.

Harold's Stones

Three standing stones
Location: 8km south of Monmouth (SO 499 051)
Access: Visible from nearby road

This site, one of the more substantial megalithic monuments in Monmouthshire is located close to the village of Trelleck. From Monmouth, head south along the B4293 towards Chepstow. Approximately 8km along this road is the village of Trelleck. The stones are in a field on the left, about 200m south of the village.

Harold's Stones is an alignment of three stones of varying height (2.5m, 3.2m and 4m). Once erect, all three stones are now leaning. Bronze Age in date, Houlder (1978, 139) speculates that they once formed part of a much larger and impressive alignment, though Castleden (1992, 387) suggests that they do not form part of a stone circle. Two cupmarks are present on the southern face of the central stone.

The sun dial of 1689 in the village church, with a carving of the three stones

An anonymous writer in *Cymru Fu* of 1890 points out that a fourth stone was standing on nearby common land, but this was destroyed during the latter part of the eighteenth century. If this account is true, then the Harold's Stones would have been a site of truly monumental form, similar to the stone rows of Dartmoor,

*There are two cup marks in the lower half of the right-hand face,
towards the left side, on the above stone*

Exmoor and western Scotland. A sundial made in 1689 in the nearby village church has the three stones carved on a supporting plinth; the numbers 8, 10 and 14 are visible on each stone which probably represented their then height in feet.

The first description of this monument was by Edward Llwyd in 1698 who referred to the stones as being 'pitched on end'. An exaggerated line-illustration of the stones accompanies the text. Kelly's *Directory of Monmouthshire and South Wales* of 1814 suggests that the stones commemorate King Harold's defeat of the Britons. On a similar theme, John Yonge Akerman in 1847 refers to the stones as the point where three chieftains fell in battle alongside Harold during campaigns against the Welsh. Earlier, in 1821, G.A. Cook suggested the stones were of druidic origin and that the place name of Trelleck means Three (Tri) Flat Stones (Llech). The first acknowledgement that the Harold's Stones are of prehistoric origin is made by Arthur Morris, who in 1905 suggested that the monument dated well before the time of Harold.

The Bronze Age

Consolidation and expansion

Venturing further than their Neolithic predecessors, Bronze Age people were not inhibited by the barrenness of the uplands to the north such as the Black Mountains. Indeed, many of the monuments dated to the Bronze Age—round barrows, cairns, standing stones and stone circles—are located on the highest points within the landscape and many are distributed within northern Monmouthshire, close to the coal mining towns of Tredegar, Beaufort, Ebbw Vale and Brynmawr. Numerous lithic scatters have been found within the upland zones to the north. A fine example of a flint knife was doscovered at Grwyne Fawr in the Black Mountains during road construction. However, our Bronze Age ancestors were also interested in exploiting the fertile lowland areas of Monmouthshire, in particular the river valleys and the lands by the Severn Estuary. Here, archaeologists have uncovered a series of settlements linked by brushwood trackways (ST 43 84 and ST 44 85) close to the present coastline at Porton Grounds and south of the small town of Magor. Within a 2km stretch of the present shore near Chapel Farm is a settlement and trackways extending southwards into what is now open water. These Caldicot Levels, now a mosaic of modern drainage channels, are very different from what they were 4,000 years ago, when the area would have been very wet and boggy, with many islands dotted around the marshes. (A similar example of this change in the landscape can be seen some 20km to the south, in the Somerset Levels.) Further west is the site of recent excavations at Goldcliff (ST 373 819). The majority of artefacts recovered were Iron Age, but there was also a substantial Bronze Age long house. Further west again, just south of Newport, where the Afon Ebbw and the Usk meet, a Bronze Age inhumation was discovered (ST 316 843) as a result of industrial development.

Monuments of this nature are usually clustered, with as many as four round barrows within a few hundred metres of each other, forming what is known as a barrow cemetery. This is similar in distribution, but not in density, to the barrows on Salisbury Plain in Wiltshire. The most visible of the cemeteries today are the three round barrows 2km east of Risca (ST 25 90) and the four (ST 25 92) clustered close to the Twm Barlwm hillfort (ST 244 927). Other clusters, although less dense, lie further north on the eastern ridges of the Black Mountains.

*Cist and cairn above Llanthony Priory in the
Black Mountains*

Close to Y Gaer Llwyd burial chamber, is the Bronze Age ritual complex of Gray Hill (ST 43 93). Here there are five round barrows, one standing stone and two stone circles, all within a square kilometre, located on a south-facing slope and overlooking two more round barrows at Trewen (ST 45 90), and the single Crick round barrow north of Caldicot, approximately 3km to the south (ST 484 903). Although all eight round barrows are of similar size and shape, they may indicate two separate social, political and symbolic ideologies. The Gray Hill complex can be considered an upland distribution, while Trewen and Crick are lowland monuments. We suggest that lowland barrows are earlier and may represent a transitional form between the long barrow tradition of the Neolithic and the complexity of the upland barrows.

The location of finds is also interesting, in that these are evenly distributed throughout the county, with the exception of the very far north-east around the village of Llantilio Crossenny, where only a couple have been recorded. Hoards containing prestige goods such as bronze socketed axes and palstaves, though few, are commonest in the north-west of the county, two examples being the Princetown hoard (SO 11 10) close to the county border of Monmouthshire and Mid-Glamorgan and the hoard at Rassau (SO 16 12). Neither these nor many of the find spots in this area are close to round barrows or related Bronze Age monuments. This picture may well be distorted as many finds are the result of excavation and building and therefore subject to chance. In the east, 4km or so south-east of Abergavenny, two hoards, one at Llanddewi Rhydderch (SO 34 13) the other at Llanvihangel Gobion (34 09), follow a similar pattern to the hoards in the north-west of the county. It would appear that Bronze Age people were drawn to the extreme upland and wetland areas of Monmouthshire in the north and west. What the attraction was is debatable, but rather than seeking economic stability in the fertile lowlands in the east and south, Bronze Age people, out of what appeared to be ritual and symbolic motives, were drawn to the mountains and related lowlands.

In some ways the distribution and ideology is similar to that of Neolithic burial monuments. However, Bronze Age monuments extend higher up the slope, an area we suggest was strictly taboo during the Neolithic. Associated with the round barrows and cairns are standing stones, which arguably could be Neolithic in date. Many of these have been destroyed or are recumbent, and all we now see is a vestige of a complex symbolic Bronze Age landscape.

Standing stones are found in both upland and lowland locations. Many are close to or on the flood plains of major river courses, whilst others are located on or near upland mountain valleys, such as the standing stone at Bedd y Gwr Hir (SO 246 134) and the examples on Gray Hill. They are far too infrequent to make any overall generalisations as to their purpose.

Two unusual standing stones, which exceed all records for size, should be mentioned. The massive Druidstone (ST 241 834), near Cardiff, is by far the largest single block of stone used for this type of monument within Monmouthshire. Standing approximately three metres high, the stone is buried to a similar depth below ground. Much farther to the north-east, just outside the village of Trelleck, are the Harold's Stones (SO 499 052), three column-like stones of varying height which appear to have been part of a much larger linear complex. Due to their size and alignment, we would suggest they resemble some of the stone alignments found elsewhere in the west of Britain (in particular, Dartmoor) and, therefore, are possibly late Neolithic, as are possibly the two known stone circles found within the county.

These circles are located close to high points. One is on the south-facing slope of Gray Hill (ST 438 935), some 260m above sea level, with a second possible circle close by. The second known stone circle lies on Garn Wen (SO 281 255), 510m above sea level and dominates a ridge overlooking the southern part of the Afon Honddu valley.

Beakers, burials and belonging

Towards the end of the Neolithic period a new burial ideology emerged, often, although not always, associated with individual inhumations under round barrows. These earthen structures are among the most conspicuous Bronze Age relics in Monmouthshire. On the mountain tops to the west and north of the county, similar monuments known as cairns occur, built of stone rather than of earth. Cairns and barrows replaced the large, austere, group monuments of the Neolithic, such as Gaer Llwyd and Thornwell Farm, which were blocked up and abandoned. Barrows and cairns, unlike the majority of Neolithic tombs which occupy the intermediate slopes, are located either on the tops of hills or on the valley floor, close to the flood plain. This change in burial practice did not necessarily entail a dramatic overthrow of the old order, but rather reflected a gradual change in the way the individual was perceived. The graves of prominent males became associated with symbols of

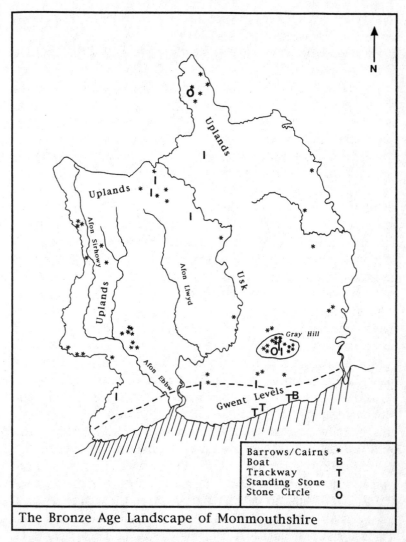

Barrows/Cairns	*
Boat	B
Trackway	T
Standing Stone	I
Stone Circle	O

The Bronze Age Landscape of Monmouthshire

hunting, warring, fighting and personal prestige, and burial practice in general seems to place less emphasis upon esoteric knowledge and secrecy than was the case during the Neolithic. Stanford has highlighted a degree of continuity between the Neolithic and succeeding Beaker period, suggesting that 'some important Neolithic locations remained the foci of activity with old routes still in use' (Stanford, 1991, 25). Certainly, sherds have been found in some chambered tombs, indicating re-use of these monuments during the Beaker phase.

The vessels from which the Beaker phase takes its name have come to stand for the new warrior idiom which characterised society from c.2,500 BC. They begin to appear in later Neolithic burial contexts and occur as part of a cultural package which includes barbed and tanged arrowheads, perforated stone plaques— sometimes known as 'archer's wristguards'—flint and metal daggers and belt rings. It was once believed this package of material symbols was introduced to Britain by invaders from the Rhine—the so-called Beaker Folk. Now, however, it is more readily accepted that the invasion was one of ideas, rather than of actual peoples. The earliest beakers were the finest and it is probable that these were imported. Thereafter the standard declined, with local copies becoming much more prevalent. The social role of beakers was clearly very important and they may have been linked to some kind of drinking cult involving the consumption of mead and barley-beer. It has been suggested (Hodder, 1990, 268) that the finer wares were linked to the wild through the natural process of fermentation, again emphasising the warrior ideal.

Monmouthshire has been dismissed as a 'a sort of Beaker no-man's land', (Barnett, 1964, 115). However, in 1964, a typical Beaker stone cist was discovered at Beachley, on the Monmouthshire-Gloucestershire border, by workmen digging a cesspit. They smashed through the capstone, which measured 1.1m by 0.7m, and only halted when they discovered the skeleton of a 19-year-old (no indication of sex is given) which was crouched in typical Beaker fashion and which appeared to have been orientated north/south. With no archaeological supervision, the remains, consisting of broken long bones and an incomplete skull, were removed and presented to a pathologist, who declared them to be 'over a hundred years old'. The skeleton was subsequently deposited in Newport Museum. Although no beaker was recovered, the form of the burial is linked to the Beaker ideology, an interpretation later confirmed by Herbert Savory (1982). Furthermore, there was no covering mound over the inhumation, which led to the comment that 'Beaker cists along the Severn shore in Monmouthshire and Gloucestershire ... were not covered by barrows' (Barnett, 1964,

115). Two cist burials of similar form have been found within the Olchon Valley, in south-west Herefordshire. They, too, lacked a covering mound. However, the grave goods, consisting of a Beaker and a barbed and tanged arrowhead, suggest the occupant of one of the cists, which has been reconstructed in Hereford City Museum, was of high status. Within Monmouthshire, barbed and tanged arrowheads have been found at Welsh Newton (SO 484 185), Dixton (SO 517 153) and Little Womas (SO 477 113).

The most frequently visualised form of social organisation for this period is the chiefdom (Service, 1962), which has at its centre a privileged figure, a kind of 'tribal banker', as a leading anthropologist has put it, receiving tribute from the local population and redistributing this income in the form of communal feasting. Such lavish displays of 'generosity' have more recently been recorded in Amazonia, the north-west coast region of North America and Papua New Guinea. The phenomenon has been interpreted as a means of building up 'a capital of obligations and debts which will be repaid in the form of homage, respect, loyalty, and, when the opportunity arises, work and services,' (Bourdieu, 1977, 195). Such 'endless conversion of economic capital into symbolic capital' (ibid.) would, at the cost of considerable time and effort, have consolidated the status of chiefs in positions of permanent domination. They would thus have been well-placed to mobilise and co-ordinate labour for the construction of a new range of monuments which appeared during the third millennium BC. In addition to barrows and cairns, these include standing stones, ring-ditches and stone circles. Metal, and particularly access to fine metalwork, would have played a key role in the process of social ferment which appears to characterise the Early Bronze Age. Such prestige goods would have acted as symbols of power and strengthened the social position of chiefs, whilst also providing a medium of exchange which facilitated interaction among neighbouring groups and opened other channels of communication, such as the exchange of marriage partners.

The Beaker phase constitutes a prelude to the Bronze Age proper, during which a complex ritual landscape evolved in Monmouthshire, as in other parts of Britain. Monuments and their surroundings were used to express an ideology seemingly bound up in the liminality of death. That is, transitional spaces were created through which the human remains passed on their journey from the living world to the realm of the dead. Just as in the Neolithic, death rituals seemed to have involved the physical movement of bodies around the landscape, such that the journey from life to death was a real one enacted in time and space. Monuments such as stone circles, we suggest, were closely linked, spatially and symbolically, with the numerous burial barrows and cairns which appeared during the Bronze Age. In seeking to move away from the interpretation of stone circles as prehistoric observatories, we would see them as integral to an archaeology of death, such that, in creating a liminal space, they prepared the deceased for the journey to its final resting place. The path from stone circle to burial mound may thus have served as a kind of processional route.

When researching the Bronze Age monuments of Herefordshire for the first volume in this series, we noted two patterns. Firstly, it is rare to find monuments individually sited within the landscape. Bronze Age barrows and cairns almost always occurred in clusters of two or more. Secondly, these clusters were usually associated either with standing stones or, in some rare cases, stone circles. Within Monmouthshire a similar pattern is apparent. We have taken one area, that of Gray Hill, and attempted to reconstruct the Bronze Age landscape.

The Gray Hill complex, a few kilometres north of Caerleon, lies on a south-facing slope overlooking the Severn Estuary and has the highest concentration of monuments dating from this period. In addition, Crick and Trewen barrows lie nearby and to the south. To the north, and now in dense managed woodland, are the two Wentwood barrows. All the sites lie within a 10 kilometre square area and are intervisible, vegetation permitting, be they lowland, on intermediate slopes or in upland locations. The positioning of each monument appears to be a deliberate statement within the landscape. All have commanding views to the south, across the southern extent of the Caldicot Levels, and over the Bristol Channel to the Quantock Hills and, to the south-west, Exmoor. Similar landscape positioning of identical stone monuments can be found on Exmoor, and the Gray Hill complex may be replicating this.

Today the landscape of Gray Hill is of heath scrub with intermittent dwarf shrubs, but during the Bronze Age, much of the area would have been farmed, in particular, the intermediate south-facing slope and the fertile lowland (to the Caldicot Levels). On the upper slopes, however, and towards the summit of Gray Hill, the social and symbolic becomes ever more privileged. For close to these upper slopes is a series of monuments consisting of three standing stones (one recumbent), two stone circles and a cemetery of perhaps five barrows. The monuments are dispersed within a network of linear and possibly contemporary turf-stoned boundaries.

The use of the barrows is quite obvious—they are burial mounds. But what of the three standing stones and the two stone circles? Traditional ideas suggest the latter may be prehistoric observatories, and the stones orientated towards the midwinter sunrise. But we would disagree and would argue that the standing stones are ritual markers within a complex landscape for they appear as a linear arrangement orientated towards the barrow cemetery approximately 300m to the north. The linearity of the monuments suggests a 'path' between the stone circle and the barrows. The latter are clearly the final resting place for the dead; the stone circle therefore may represent the beginning of that death—a space where the dead could be viewed, a form of lying in state before interment. Within the circle, the space is special and sacred and very different from that directly outside and down the slope. The standing stones may be seen as demarcating the processional route of the deceased. These markers within the landscape would, therefore, signify a spatial as well as a chronological journey to the after-life.

The Gray Hill complex may have served a number of uses in addition to that of burial. For instance, inextricably linked with death is rebirth. In many hunter-gatherer societies, ritual is controlled by the elders, and trinkets belonging to ancestors may be passed on. In Madagascar today the dead are temporarily interred in communal tombs where they are wrapped in a ceremonial cloth, known as a lambre. Newly married couples related to the dead then use this cloth to copulate on—the idea is that even in death, life is created.

Many contemporary tribal societies use a certain place or space to signify a transition, say, between juvenile and adult (rites of passage). Such liminal space may appear in many forms: a tunnel, a complete landscape outside the village bounds or, in the case of Early Bronze Age Monmouthshire, a circular space demarcated by stone. It might appear far-fetched that an individual experiencing the ritual change from juvenile to adult should undergo his or her rite of passage by following the path through life to death—from the stone circle to the barrow. But this idea is not as implausible as one might imagine. Within our own society many people are christened, confirmed, married and buried from within the same ritual complex—the church. It could be that the ritual complex of Gray Hill, like the Christian church, took on many functions, all of them linked to the life cycle.

Farming the lowland, grazing the upland

Although Bronze Age communities relied heavily on the fertile soils of the lowlands and intermediate slopes, many Monmouthshire barrows are located in the uplands. The way these barrows are organised into linear groups, usually taking advantage of upland scarps, suggests that tribal groups were organised into social territories and skirmishes or minor conflicts may have broken out over possession of prime agricultural land in the fertile lowlands. It is important to note that large-scale agriculture was adopted as the main economy during this period and not during the Neolithic. Neolithic communities continued to rely heavily on seasonal hunting, gathering, foraging and fishing and their agriculture, according to pollen analysis, consisted merely of allotment-style gardening.

The Bronze Age agricultural system seems to have been expansive, for the pollen record reveals that, after about 1,700 BC, woodland clearance intensified. Increasingly marginal soils, those over 300m above sea level, came under the plough, whilst Early Bronze Age monuments at very high elevations may indicate seasonal occupation and exploitation of this highest land. Another new feature of the archaeological record is the field boundary. Aerial photography suggests the existence of boundaries and ringed enclosures which are contemporary with the barrow tradition on land near Merthyr Tydfil. These indicate increasing concern with land ownership and allocation.

The Early Bronze Age was a relatively warm and dry period, with oak and alder woodland dominating much of the lowland landscape. It was a climate well suited to the spread of cereal cultivation. During the Middle Bronze Age, however, the weather became increasingly cool and wet. Upland farms colonised a few generations earlier would have become untenable owing to this climatic deterioration. There would not have been enough summer warmth to ripen wheat and barley, while excessive rainfall would have led to the over-development of plants and weakening of the straw. Furthermore, the wetter climate caused the formation of blanket peat in the uplands of north-west Monmouthshire, where the soils would soon have become barren and useless to farmers. The social effects of this climatic shift meant that new lowland areas were exploited, leading to increased forest clearance to create new ploughland and pasture.

As a result of agricultural expansion, more and more tribute, in the form of food and possibly textiles, would have been channelled towards the centre of local systems, increasing the prosperity of chiefs and their ability to participate in a wider arena of gift exchange. At first flint, then copper, gold and finally bronze (an alloy of 90 per cent copper with 10 per cent tin) would have been central to this exchange process. The kinds of prestige items that would have circulated in Monmouthshire during the Early Bronze Age are not known, but elsewhere flat axes, flanged axes and daggers have dominated the finds, along with gold torcs and drinking vessels.

The Later Bronze Age: the power of exchange
After about 1,500 BC, bronze forms such as the palstave, an unwieldy hourglass-shaped axe, and the socketed axe proliferated in Monmouthshire. Indeed, the palstave is one of the commonest Bronze Age finds in the county with at least 22 examples, found mainly in the east near Usk, Raglan, Bassaleg, Monmouth, Chepstow and Abergavenny. These would no doubt have been exchanged between members of an hierarchical society obsessed with showing off their wealth. The intricacy of design, coupled with changes in type suggests that the craftsmanship involved was restricted to certain members of a structured hierarchical society. Evidence of hoards within the county leads to the idea that in time of conflict or political instability, owners of such hoards felt it

Late Bronze Age socketed axe with rib decoration,
found at Llanfoist

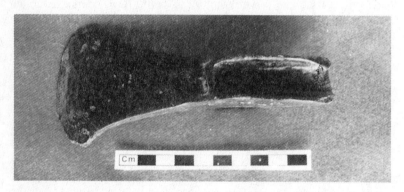

Middle Bronze Age unlooped palstave axe,
found during ploughing at Blaengavenny Farm

necessary to bury their wealth. The larger and more decorative the item, the more power it would represent. Four types of palstave are known in Monmouthshire: blade only, unlooped, single looped and ribbed. In the early and middle Bronze Age, prestige goods tended to end up in the graves of high-ranking people, mainly male burials. Towards the later Bronze Age, however, the evidence suggests they were either buried or thrown into rivers and lakes, possibly as offerings to water deities. Such intentional destruction of wealth finds a parallel in the potlatch system of the north-west Coastal American Indians. Here, status is augmented through the destruction of valuables. In one sense, this is the final disposal of outdated or unfashionable prestige items, and, in another sense, it is a way of returning them back from whence they came. Either way, the item is being given, and Marcel Mauss (1954) has suggested that in some societies the more one gave, the more powerful one became.

Interestingly, finds of this later period are distributed within an area of Monmouthshire where there are few barrows, and it was probably at this time that the idea of burial in high-status monuments such as barrows and cairns fell out of fashion. We know that towards the beginning of the Iron Age territory was marked out by hillforts, and monuments to the dead all but disappear from the landscape. This change in ideology coincides with the abandonment of barrows and cairns throughout the county. It is worth noting that in west Wales, Bronze Age hillforts have been identified.

This shift in ideology broadly coincides with an increase in weaponry and armour, the latter making use of the new sheet metal working techniques, whilst a surge in output of general bronzework may indicate the metal was being used much more for tools, such as sickles. Prestige bronzes were still produced, though some of the finer pieces were perhaps the work of travelling smiths who sold their services to the highest bidder. Socketed axes are probably our final reminder of the old system of prestige goods, and these continued to be produced into the Iron Age. Finds of socketed axes, both single and double looped are distributed in large numbers throughout the county. Indeed, a group of socketed axes form part of a hoard found at Rassau. Lower grade items such as dress pins and working axes and sickles were probably manufactured and distributed locally.

A fascinating glimpse of later Bronze Age daily life has been revealed by recent excavations at Caldicot Castle. The site lies within a country park, some 1.5km from the present coastline and within the town boundary. It is hardly known outside archaeological circles, yet it has revealed an almost complete environmental record for the Bronze Age, including a wooden trackway and one of Europe's finest and earliest plank-clad boats. The site was dug during the late 1980s and early 90s and revealed a 20m wide creek. Five distinct phases were identified, beginning with post-hole structures and the foundation for a trackway; a later wooden platform; an abandonment phase; a brushwood track phase and finally a second brushwood track phase.

The environmental data and the boat were well preserved in rich estuarine organic clays. The boat was built of oak and was crafted using an axe, shafted as an adze-type tool. Also present were the cutting marks of the carpenter. Large planks, up to 2m in length, had been cut with metal axes and laid to make a track-way across a reed swamp. Also present was a large quantity of daily items, including pottery, flint, animal bone, metalwork and a large amount of charcoal. Sifting through the household waste has opened a window onto Bronze Age life; bones recovered included those of horse, cattle, sheep, pig, red deer, brown hare, water vole and large quantities of wild fowl, especially mallard. Environmental data included a log which bore the toothmarks of European beaver. A radiocarbon date of 940+/-70 BC was taken from peat deposits and places the second phase, that of the wooden platform, firmly within the Late Bronze Age.

Llangybi Bottom Stone

> Standing stone 1.8m high
> Location: 4km south of Usk (ST 380 963)
> Access: Visible from nearby track

From Usk proceed west towards Pontypool across the bridge and take the immediate left towards Caerleon. Approximately 4km down this road is the village of Llangybi. From the village take a sharp left, pass the church and continue for about 600m. There is a Dŵr Cymru pumping station on the right. Continue along the track marked 'No Access' for approximately 700m. The Llangybi Stone is clearly visible standing in a large open meadow about 300m on the right.

This standing stone follows a similar pattern in design and landscape positioning to many others in Monmouthshire. Firstly, like the Druidstone and Llanfihangel Rogiet stone, the monument is pointed. The eastern edge of the upper part of the stone has been sheared off, yet we are convinced the stone was originally worked to a point. The position, close to water, is also similar to that of other lowland standing stones. The stone stands 1.8m high and is oriented south-east/north-west. It is of conglomerated sandstone, the material used for many other standing stones in Monmouthshire.

Surprisingly, the monument appears to be isolated, although there is a possible stone circle 2km to the south-west, close to the hamlet of Llwyncelyn, and Bronze Age finds, including flint, have been found between two and three kilometres to the south. Comparison with other sites both in Monmouthshire and Herefordshire suggests that there were once barrows on the river meadows.

Gray Hill Complex

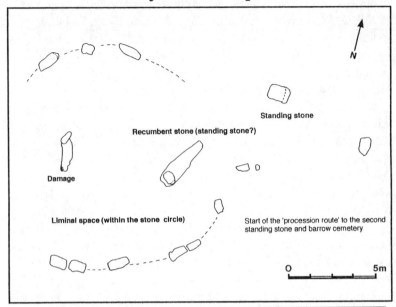

A stone circle 9.8m in diameter, with a possible second stone circle to the west; three standing stones, one of which is recumbent; a barrow cemetery and field systems
Location: 5km north-west of Caldicot. The Stone Circle is at ST 438 935, and the barrow cemetery at ST 441 932
Access: Public paths circle the hill, and other paths lead across the hilltop

Consisting of bracken moorland and with a dense concentration of monuments, Gray Hill is regarded as one of the most important Bronze Age landscapes in the whole of Monmouthshire. Like the spatial and hierarchical ordering of standing stones and barrows on the edge of the Gwent Levels, the Gray Hill monuments appear to be organised so as to be seen from a distance and to be intervisible with each other. We would argue that each monument is the site of one stage in a procession which is symbolically and ritualistically controlled. Earlier in the text we suggested the procession may be linked to burial and/or initiation.

As one approaches the summit of Gray Hill, the first monuments to appear are the two standing stones and the stone circle, which Burl (1977, 370) describes as a cairn circle. Beyond these, and on a ridge to the north, is the barrow cemetery. Possible localised quarrying on top of the hill confuses the picture somewhat, though a series of field boundaries, which may be contemporary or slightly later, does not appear to intercut the Bronze Age monuments to any extent.

Several of the original stones have been removed from the circle since 1868, but 13 visible rectangular stones are left, some of which stand 0.5m high. Others have fallen and lie flat, but remain within the ring. It has been suggested (by CADW) that a possible cist or burial chamber exists inside the circle on the south-east side. When visiting the site in April 1996, we could not see any evidence of this. Indeed, few stone circles from this part of western Britain possess either a cist or a burial chamber. However, it may have been that during the early Bronze Age some stone circles were re-used by constructing a mound within the inner structure. The large barrow on Exmoor, known as Setta Barrow (SS 726 381), has around its diameter a series of upright stones or kerbing. These may have been set up prior to the monument's use as a barrow.

A large standing stone which may have stood centrally within the Gray Hill circle now lies recumbent to the south-east. Surrounding the stone circle is a slightly undulating area of ground, suggesting the monument may once have been ringed by a circular bank and ditch as in a henge. To the east is a standing stone approximately 1.8m high. This would appear to mark the beginning of the processional way to the top of the hill. Approximately 50-60m beyond the standing stone and stone circle is another standing stone, 2.1m high. Both are orientated north-south and, according to Whittle, may be set in line with the midwinter sunrise. However, both of these monuments and the standing stone appear to the authors to be oriented towards the barrow cemetery, the terminal point of the procession route. Here, the Sites and Monuments Record has recently recognised a series of 12 cairns and barrows organised into three groups and dispersed along the northern, southern and eastern ridges of Gray Hill (ST 440 932 and 441 932).

The landscape potential of this complex is considerable. Views to the south incorporate the upland ridges to the Gwent Levels, the

Bristol Channel and the uplands of Exmoor and the Quantock Hills. Viewed from the lowland barrows and standing stones, Gray Hill acts as a focal point within the landscape. The spatial relationship of monuments appears to be similar in both uplands and lowlands, the Gray Hill complex repeating the landscape distribution below.

The south standing stone near Gray Hill stone circle, part of the processional route to the barrows

Llanfihangel Rogiet Standing Stone

A 1.9m high standing stone
Location: 3km west of Caldicot (ST 445 877)
Access: Can be seen from the B4245

From junction 23 of the M4 take the B4245 east towards Caldicot. The standing stone is found approximately 1km beyond Magor, just before Llanfihangel Rogiet church. Located close to the recently-constructed second Severn Bridge trunk road, this monument stands proud against recent disturbance and the destruction of its landscape setting to the east.

Formed from conglomerated sandstone, and standing approximately 1.9m high, this stone is similar in shape to that of the Llangybi stone and the larger Druidstone. Around its base there is evidence of cattle-trample and disturbed packing. Now fenced off with barbed wire, the stone has been allowed to become overgrown with wetland grasses. During the Bronze Age it would have demarcated the landscape so as to divide the social and domestic to the south, from the symbolic to the north. Located at the foot of the northern extent of the Caldicot Levels, this monument may have been visually aligned with the settlements south of Magor Pill. Here, a series of trackways and footprints, believed to be Bronze Age and Mesolithic respectively, indicates there could have been continual use of the landscape for at least 3,000 years. There have been a few chance finds of Bronze Age flint either side of the standing stone, whilst about 3.5km to the east is the trackway and recently-discovered boat which date from the same period. It is also arguable that the monument forms part of a ritual landscape that includes the Gray Hill complex and it is interesting to note that there appear to be four levels of social/ritual/symbolic activity within the area. Firstly, settlement is located either on, or close to, the shores of the Severn Estuary. Several kilometres beyond this is a line of standing stones which runs along the southern extent of a ridge dividing the Caldicot Levels from the uplands. Approximately 2km farther north is a line of barrows, and beyond them the ritual landscape of Gray Hill.

The Druidstone

The largest of Monmouthshire's standing stones
Location: To the north-east of Cardiff (ST 241 834)
Access: By permission from the owners of Druidstone House
in whose grounds it stands

The Druidstone is by far the largest of all Monmouthshire's standing stones. The size and shape of the stone have given rise to many folk tales—legend has it that at midnight, when a cock crows, the stone will uproot itself and go down to the Afon Rhymni.

Located in the private grounds of Druidstone House, near Castleton, permission must be sought from the owners when visiting this site. From junction 28 on the M4, take the A48 south-west towards Cardiff to the village of Castleton, a distance of about 3.5km. In Castleton take the first turning to the right, signposted 'Michaelston'. Continue along this road for approximately 1km and take the second left. Druidstone House lies about 500m along this road on the left. Beware of the dogs!

The monument forms part of a series of standing stones occupying the lowlands of southern Monmouthshire. This enormous stone stands 3.2m high, though the height during the Bronze Age may have been even greater, for soil appears to have been fairly recently banked against the base.

Close by, and dwarfing the stone, are garden trees and shrubs, including a large copper beech. Observation of the surrounding landscape is obscured by Druidstone House, other neighbouring houses and trees. The stone's location appears to be deliberate for, sited on a large ridge running east-west, it would have offered uninterrupted views to the Bristol Channel during the Late Neolithic and Early Bronze Age. During this period, the channel would have been much narrower than at present.

The shape of the monument is comparable with that of other standing stones along the Gwent Levels in that they all taper to a point. Furthermore, all are of conglomerated sandstone.

Twyn-Yr-Oerfel Round Barrows & Twyn Cae Hugh Barrow

> A series of barrows
> Location: 4km north-west of Caerphilly
> (ST 181 907, ST 185 905 & ST 174 915)
> Access: They lie alongside public footpaths

From Caerphilly, take the A468 to the small town of Machen. Just inside the town boundary, take the second left and head along a narrow, steep country lane for approximately 6km. The lane from this point is unmetalled. The first two barrows are sited alongside this track and are clearly visible. About 1.8km to the north-west is the Twyn Cae Hugh barrow. Here the road becomes more uneven, and hazardous in places, so proceed with caution—or park and walk!

Located on the highest points in the landscape, each commands views over the Sirhowy Valley to the east. The Twyn Cae Hugh barrow, now located on the edge of forestry land, is by far the best preserved of the three.

All three barrows exhibit the classic 'doughnut' hollowing which indicates they have been plundered by antiquarians. At Twyn Cae Hugh, recent digging within the south-west area of the hollowing, possibly resulting from people using metal detectors, has revealed a little of the internal construction. Beneath the outer earthen skin of the mound is a carefully constructed interwoven drystone frame. It is suggested that the other two barrows are similarly constructed, making use of the most abundant material in the vicinity—stone.

Crick Round Barrow

A round barrow
Location: 1.5km north of Caldicot (ST 484 902)
Access: can be viewed from nearby road

From junction 24 on the M4, take the A48 signposted 'Chepstow'. Approximately 14km along this road is the village of Crick. Just before passing under a railway bridge, the Crick barrow can be seen in a triangular field north of the road. From the gate, the low mound is visible approximately 50m to the north-west.

This is one of the largest barrows in Monmouthshire and has been subjected to much antiquarian investigation. Despite its importance, however, it has suffered the ravages of intensive agriculture. Standing less than a metre high, the mound has spread over the still-visible kerbing. In the centre is the tell-tale 'doughnut' effect of previous excavation. Crick is unique among mounds in Monmouthshire, though is similar to Setta Barrow on Exmoor, in that both have pronounced kerbing around the perimeter. It is suggested that it may be the site of an earlier monument, possibly dating to the Late Neolithic, and that the stones delineate some crude circular structure. In order to give it special burial significance, we propose that the site was later transformed into a barrow.

This is one of a series of barrows with a lowland landscape position. It has been suggested that it is later than barrows and cairns sited in upland areas (Children & Nash, 1994, 57). Close by, to the west, there are at least three other barrows which possibly all form an extended linear barrow cemetery positioned along the top of a ridge overlooking the Caldicot Levels. During the Bronze Age all four barrows would have been intervisible. Still further west is the standing stone at Langstone. Again, this is sited on a ridge. One can therefore suggest that all monuments along this ridge may have been used as processional (and political) markers within the landscape, similar to those of nearby Gray Hill, 5km to the north.

Wentwood Round Barrows

> Two round barrows
> Location: 9km north-west of Newport (ST 416 945)
> Access: They lie alongside a forestry track

From junction 24 on the M4, take the A48 to Chepstow. Approximately 9km along this road make a left turn onto a road signposted 'Parc-Seymour'. Head north for approximately 5.7km towards the small hamlet of Pen y cae-mawr. Near the top of the hill in Wentwood, and about 1km before reaching the hamlet, take a right hand turning onto an unmetalled forestry track. Both monuments are clearly visible about 250m from the turning and 10m north of the track.

These two large monuments stand on the top of Wentwood Ridge, and would have overlooked the barrows on the northern ridge of Gray Hill. The eastern barrow is the largest, but both have been heavily damaged by four-wheel drive vehicles. Other damage includes tree-rooting, the result of extensive planting during the nineteenth century. Tree roots have infiltrated all areas of both mounds. However, on the positive side, there appears to be no central hollowing on either mound, suggesting that any cists within the barrows remain intact.

During the Bronze Age, these barrows and the barrow complex on Gray Hill would have been intervisible. Indeed, these could be regarded as satellites of the Gray Hill monuments, similar to the lowland ridge monuments located to the south (close to the A48 and M4). It could well have been the case that procession was as important from the north as it was from the south. Beyond the two barrows, approximately 7km to the north-west, is the Llangybi standing stone and this pattern of standing stone/barrow/stone circle is repeated in the south. We should also note that Gray Hill is roughly the same height as Wentwood Ridge—between 260m and 300m above sea level. To the north and north-west, there is no evidence of any Bronze Age activity. One can argue, therefore, that the Wentwood barrows, in addition to being tombs, are symbolic landscape markers.

Middle Hendre Round Barrow

A round barrow
Location: 6km west of Monmouth (SO 454 138)
Access: Can be viewed from the road

From Monmouth, proceed west along the B4233 towards Abergavenny. Approximately 6km along this road, some 3km past the hamlet of Rockfield, take the first left signposted 'Llanvihangel-Ystern-Llewern'. The Middle Hendre round barrow stands 1km from the turning in a field on the right. It is opposite a T junction with a country lane.

This monument, a lowland earthen barrow, is one of a small number located in the east of the county. Very little in the way of flint, metal hoards and cairns have been found in the vicinity.

The Iron Age

During the Iron Age hillforts replaced ritual centres as expressions of local identity, and some attained truly monumental dimensions. They seem to have served agricultural hinterlands as focal points—perhaps initially as meeting places. But their precise role in Iron Age society is still very much a matter of archaeological debate. What is certain, however, is that the term 'fort' carries meanings which are too narrowly militaristic. To argue that they were constructed purely for defence is to leave out of account the impact that hillforts would have had as statements of social identity within the 'tribal' society of Iron Age Britain. Unlike earlier periods of prehistory, the Iron Age landscape was not demarcated by monuments associated with death. Yet hillforts—the major public works of their day—would have communicated powerful symbolic meanings.

From the Late Bronze Age onwards the landscape was principally an agricultural one, consisting of settlements and fields. These were surrounded by grazing land or scrub, while beyond lay the natural environment—the wildwood—which man exploited as a predator in search of game, or as a gatherer of fruits and timber. This landscape would not have been a neutral backdrop to human action, but rather bound up with histories and myths—accounts and stories of how the world came to be as it was. Such stories would have ordered and personified the physical environment of mountains, rivers, lakes and forests. By so doing they would have helped create a familiarity with the environment, an unquestioning apprehension of the world, a sense of belonging. Stories may have incorporated earlier monuments—Neolithic burial chambers and Bronze

Age barrows, stone circles and standing stones—just as more recent folklore has attempted to interpret these and Iron Age features by weaving together myth and magic with known people and events.

The people who created this landscape are generally termed 'Celts'. According to early historical references, they were impetuous and quick to take offence—a 'warrior' people given to arrogant self-display. Cultural maps of Late Iron Age Britain based upon the textual evidence available show a mosaic of Celtic 'tribal' territories. Monmouthshire would have fallen within the territory of the Silures, described by Tacitus (who believed they had originated in the Iberian peninsula), as dark-skinned and curly-haired and quite different in appearance from other British peoples. Too often, however, these tribal labels have been accepted uncritically as referring to enduring historical groupings, even though anthropology has shown that the concept of the 'tribe' is of dubious validity in terms of social identity and that archaeologists who adhere to it could be accused of being too heavily influenced by the more recent colonial past of western Europe. So too in their emphasis upon invasion and colonisation as the main vehicle for the transmission of Iron Age culture—an 'invasion neurosis', as the archaeologist J.G.D. Clark put it.

A.H. Williams, for example, wrote in *An Introduction to the History of Wales* that 'the practice of hillfort building is now thought to have been introduced to Wales during the last few centuries of the prehistoric era by Celtic immigrants who came here from Devon and Somerset via the Bristol Channel and the Severn Valley.' Certainly we would not deny that ideas linked to hillfort-building may have originated outside Monmouthshire, and even outside Britain. But invasions and migrations do not have to be the vehicle for the transmission of these ideas. For one thing, following the advent of radiocarbon dating, many hillforts have been shown to be far older than Williams suggests, developing from the Late Bronze Age onwards, and could not possibly have been the work of his 'Celtic immigrants'. As Stanford says: 'Whereas these camps were once viewed as a late reaction to the Roman invasion, the chronological bracket has expanded dramatically,' (1991, 43). While pre-Roman migrations are documented, there are other mechanisms such as the emulation of 'foreign' ideas by native communities, which could account for the spread of common Iron Age cultural traits.

Hillfort-building may have been adopted by these communities as a means of establishing new symbols of power at a time when bronze-related prestige had gone into decline. The emphasis upon defences may have helped sustain the ideal of warrior prowess as a central value of society, and raiding and individual display may have been important components of the ethos which developed around hillforts.

Despite the fact that Llanmelin has been identified—somewhat dubiously—as the capital of the Silures, the overall picture for Monmouthshire during this period is one of largely egalitarian social units, with no single centre dominating. We might envisage hillforts proliferating in an environment of competitive display between more or less equal neighbours, or 'peer polities'. To this extent they may be compared with the cathedrals of medieval Europe. Within each of these polities, one or more hillforts would have exerted control over the surrounding countryside. The activity of hillfort-building must have entailed a strong element of co-operation between individual families and such bonding would have helped create the social building-blocks necessary for the later large-scale resistance to Rome.

Power, people and politics

The Iron Age people of Monmouthshire enter written history towards the end of the period. They are called Silures, a tribal grouping occupying territories spanning much of present-day South Wales, and extending perhaps as far east as Herefordshire. As a 'Celtic' people they shared a reputation for stubbornness and aggression with contemporary peoples right across Europe. The Silures, however, seemed to have guarded their independence particularly forcefully. Their extreme hostility to Rome sparked a bitter and protracted struggle against domination. The leader of the Silures, and other western 'tribes', and very much the symbol of British resistance to Roman domination during the middle years of the first century AD, has come down through history and folklore as Caractacus, Caratacos or Caradoc. He led a ferocious campaign against the Roman governor, Ostorius Scapula, transferring the war from South Wales northwards to the lands of the Ordovices. The showdown with Ostorius is said by some to have taken place on the River Severn, near Newtown. Others claim the scene of Caratacos' final defeat was the hillfort of Coxall Knoll, near Leintwardine in Herefordshire. Wherever the battle was fought, it seems Caratacos and his followers were overwhelmed. His family was captured, while the resistance leader himself managed to escape, only to be betrayed to the enemy shortly afterwards by Cartimandua, a female Celtic ruler and collaborator. Despite Caratacos' capture, however, the Silures continued to oppose Rome and briefly managed to attract other 'tribes' to form an anti-Roman confederacy. They were finally subdued and romanized under the governorship of Sextus Julius Frontinus, when it is said they were moved from their 'native fortress' at Llanmelin to a new Roman town 3km away at Caerwent.

Mention of Cartimandua raises the question of the role of women in Celtic society. This was apparently complex, and social attitudes ambivalent. Lavish burials from Europe dating to 600 - 400 BC indicate they were sometimes accorded high status. Classical writers refer to prominent Celtic women, and some female rulers are mentioned by name in later centuries. There also seems to have been the sense that women were dangerous, even taboo. Powerful goddesses influenced the course of events and directed human fortunes. Other classes of women inhabited the grey, or 'liminal', area between this world and the otherworld. These were the druid-esses and seers, who possessed the power of prophecy and divina-tion; and enchantresses, who were believed to have tempted humans across the threshold separating the two 'worlds'. Ritual decapitation was a fate that befell some women, particularly the middle-aged and elderly who were identified as witches. Sometimes their lower jaw was removed in an apparently symbolic attempt to prevent them speaking, and therefore cursing, after death. Yet the evidence from other sources, such as texts of the law, indicate a mundane reality in which most women wielded little power.

In terms of language, material culture and possibly religious beliefs the Celts formed a unified pan-European culture stretching from the Carpathians in the east to the Atlantic coasts in the west.

But this apparent homogeneity probably concealed a good deal of diversity, with Celtic traits perhaps being blended with older traditions towards the Atlantic fringe of Europe and well away from developments in the heartland of the Celtic world. As D.W. Harding has observed, '... there can be little doubt that the British Iron Age from its inception retained a strong native component.' (Harding, 1974, 134).

Religion and Ritual

The scholar Miranda Green has pointed out that the Celtic world was one made up of rural communities profoundly in tune with the landscape and natural phenomena (Green, 1995). It is hardly surprising, therefore, that most Celtic deities took the form of spirits from nature. They assumed various cult forms among different Celtic communities and in this way helped to sustain a sense of local identity and belonging. One 'tribal' god of the Silures may have been named Ocelus as the feet belonging to a statue of this deity were discovered at Caerwent. Also from Caerwent is a small mother-goddess figurine which was found deep within a well. In addition to anthropomorphic deities, the Celtic imagination ascribed religious significance to birds and animals. This second group of beings includes ravens, swans, bulls, horses, stags and—among the Silures—cats. A number of tiles from Caerleon portray heads with cat-ears. Although found in a Roman context, it has been proposed that 'all would seem to be directly relevant to native, doubtless Silurian, cults, and they are unparalleled ... These strange cat-eared heads may thus reflect some genuine cult current amongst the Silures in which a deity, not necessarily to be regarded as a cat-god, at least has close affinities with cats in his cult legend, and perhaps traditionally manifests himself in feline form' (Ross, 1967, 383-4). Horned beings were particularly important in Celtic imagery and horns are given to creatures which do not naturally bear them. This class includes humans, and myths tell of shape-shifting in which people assumed the forms of animals.

Underlying many of the depictions in Celtic iconography is the profound and universal importance of the human head. Ross (1967, 95-6) believes the Celtic cult of the head is rooted in Early Bronze Age Europe 'where the head was clearly used in certain instances as a solar symbol.' In addition to artificial images of the head, the skulls of enemies were prized by Celtic warriors and seem to have been an important aspect of heroic display. The human head is often associated with sacred waters. In Welsh folklore the link between the skull and wells, perhaps regarded as entrances to the underworld, was replicated in Christian legends of the saints. For example, in Brecknockshire, when St Lludd was decapitated a spring burst forth from the rock against which the severed head came to rest. Skulls have also been found deposited in deep shafts, which, like wells, were probably regarded as entrances to the underworld. It is possible that there were also connections with fertility; a stone head found at Port Talbot has been interpreted as one of a number of 'phallic' heads.

The places where Celtic people worshipped are little known. Hogg has identified a sacred area at Maiden Castle, but in the main shrines, if they existed, must have been fairly insubstantial structures or enclosures, for they have left no trace for archaeologists to discover. They may have been located in forests, for certain species of tree are known to have been singled out for reverence, particularly the oak, and to a lesser extent, the ash and the yew. Religious rituals may have been performed at the sources of rivers, which were also revered. Such rituals appear to have been under the direction of druids, mysterious figures who have been the subject of much discussion by generations of antiquarians and romantics. They comprised the priestly class of Celtic society and appear to have monopolised sacred knowledge. As in earlier periods of prehistory and in later history, the possession of such knowledge would have been a source of power in society—power which it seems did not rest exclusively in the hands of men, for there is written evidence for the existence of female druids. The druids also seem to have played a prominent political role. It is said that in some parts of Wales they orchestrated the opposition to Rome, inspiring warriors to extreme bravery through the doctrine of the immortal soul and cultivating a belief similar to that of the Mau Mau terrorists, who were convinced of their immunity to weaponry (Harding, 1974, 101).

What might be termed secular rituals were performed—according to the early Irish texts which provide many clues to the nature of Iron Age beliefs and practices—by skilled singers or bards. Like the druids, they enjoyed high social status as people of special gifts. Theirs was an oral tradition which was only written down by scribes in the Christian era; the tradition of the bard is still celebrated in Wales at the Royal National Eisteddfod. Bardic performances seem to have been highly structured, according to set forms, and to have been composed to praise the deeds of warriors and chieftains. As Posidonius says: 'the Celts have in their company even in war ... companions [who] pronounce their praises before the whole assembly and before each of the chieftains in turn as they listen.' At the same time, enemies were reviled, while the standing of the 'tribe' (or clan) was celebrated through the invocation of its history and genealogy. To us these formulaic compositions would probably have sounded rather repetitive. As C.M. Bowra, an expert on primitive song, has observed 'repetition ... is fundamental. The theme is thought to be of such importance that it is stressed by repetition in a way that might seem to us unnecessary ...' (Bowra, 1962, 77). The words would have been only part of the whole and would probably have been accompanied by a stringed instrument and perhaps dance. The human voice was used to achieve a range of effects—for lamentation, chanting and as an instrument of war to strike terror into the hearts of foes. Chilling war cries and verbal abuse, in addition to body piercing and tattooing, would have been part of the battlefield preparation of Celtic warriors.

A third group in a triumvirate of those having special gifts were the 'seers' mentioned by several Classical authors, and said to possess the power, developed through years of training, of being able to predict the future from the death throes of sacrificial victims.

Economy

In west-central Europe from about the middle of the first millennium BC a 'prestige goods economy' developed which linked local elites directly into the Mediterranean world. Hides, slaves and agricultural commodities were exchanged for Mediterranean wine, and luxury goods manufactured in southern workshops. The economies of west-central Europe were stimulated through the acquisition of these high-status luxury goods and prestige building projects were undertaken. Around 500 BC, the Heuneberg hillfort in southern Germany was re-fortified using mud bricks—a totally unsuitable and unstable material in the moist climate of the region. Its use clearly served a symbolic function and was intended to enhance the prestige of the builders by emphasising their links with the Mediterranean. We would argue that this kind of symbolic use of architectural forms as message bearers would have played a significant role throughout the hillfort province of temperate Europe.

Beyond this west-central zone, cultures would largely have followed their own developmental paths, for groups would have traded with their neighbours, rather than directly with the Mediterranean area. A system of down-the-line exchanges along the Atlantic coast of Europe from western Britain to Iberia may have fed raw materials indirectly into the Mediterranean economy. These exchanges would have been embedded in local social systems, regulated by tradition and linked to cycles of gift and commodity exchange, perhaps in the form of seasonal 'fairs' (Hogg, 1975, 35). Exchanges may perhaps have been carried out at 'tribal' or clan boundaries, and hillforts could have played a role in this process. Accompanying the movement of goods would have been the exchange of ideas linked to hillfort-building and their elaboration.

The subsistence economy of the Iron Age people of Monmouthshire was based upon a mixture of arable farming and herding, the proportion of each probably varying with the topography and fertility of the region. The relationship between farming practices and hillfort distribution is difficult to identify. Twyn-y-Gaer in the north of the county, on the edge of the Black Mountains, has produced evidence of an early fenced enclosure which may have been used for corralling animals, and it is possible that stock-raising was a more important part of the local economy in this area. However, many of the hillforts are concentrated along the river valleys of southern Monmouthshire, where they may have served as storage points for arable crops passed up from the fertile lowlands. The Gwent Levels would have provided excellent pastures, which were no doubt as attractive to Iron Age peoples as they were to the later Roman legionary stockmen. An inscribed stone discovered at Goldcliff in 1878 may represent a boundary that existed between the legionary lands associated with Caerleon, 9km away, and those of the romanized Silures (Boon, 1980, 28).

Gradually, the consolidation of farming communities would have given rise to changes in landscape perception. Territory may have been more tightly defined, a development implied by the appearance of prominent hillforts and 'Celtic' field systems. Beyond the bounds of the cultivated and familiar, the untamed forest, while diminishing as a result of clearances, would have remained a mysterious place. So too the region's lakes and mountains, although well-worn pathways trodden by herders would have extended the 'familiar' up into the highland zone. Access to the wild may have been restricted and governed by ritual observances, imbuing gathering, and particularly hunting, with a special significance. As in medieval times, the hunt, an expression of the warrior ideal, may have been the preserve of nobles, and skill in the chase a source of prestige. But overall the products of hunting and gathering contributed relatively little to the Iron Age diet; remains indicate a reliance upon domesticated flocks and herds and upon cultivated cereals. Cattle were of such importance that they were accorded symbolic value: bulls signifying virility, while cows represented fertility. Milk and cheese, the consumption of which appears to have increased from around 3,000 BC, also formed an important part of the diet. Querns used for grinding wheat and barley have been found in large numbers on Iron Age sites, as have loom weights, which were used in weaving. Forests, as well as providing the occasional deer for the hunt, would have been a vital source of timber, the most ubiquitous building material in the Iron Age. Wood was used not only for constructing houses, but also for fences and palisades, and for trackways of the kind recently revealed on the Severn Estuary mudflats. Overall, the picture for Iron Age Monmouthshire is one of largely self-sufficient economic and political territories.

Material Culture: the expression of the 'Celtic spirit'
The so-called 'three age system' of stone, bronze and iron is extremely simplistic and unsatisfactory to many archaeologists because it imposes rigid categories upon a reality of gradual social, economic and symbolic change. The Iron Age conventionally

begins around 800 BC, but this date does not signify any kind of developmental leap in society. The use of iron began in Europe as early as 1,000 BC, yet it was not until around 600 BC that the metal came to be used for the majority of tools and weapons. Even then, bronze continued in use for decorative items. For example, recent acquisitions by Newport Museum, all dating from some time in the first century BC to the first century AD, include a bronze animal head terminal from Chepstow, a bronze lynch-pin terminal found in the Wye valley and another similar piece discovered at Raglan. The distinction between the ages is therefore blurred and the labels rather misleading. In Monmouthshire, far from the epicentre of the Celtic world, material culture retained a strong native component, with local craftspeople adapting Celtic imagery and iconography to their own traditions. The appearance of typical Celtic styles in the area should not, therefore, be taken as evidence of migration.

The Iron Age is conventionally divided into the phases Halstatt and La Tene, with the latter phase, from about 500 BC, representing the efflorescence of 'Celtic art'. In 1911, one of the most famous finds of Iron Age material in south-east Wales came to light. This was a, possibly ritual, lake deposit discovered at Llyn Fawr and dated to around 600 BC. It comprised bronze pieces and a continental iron sword. Later, daggers followed by early La Tene swords with highly decorated scabbards became fashionable. These developed into local and regional variants. Iron Age pottery is very abundant, including a range of feasting and drinking vessels. Finds of cauldron-hangers and firedogs emphasise the importance of hearths, domesticity and feasting. As for ornamentation, early Iron Age pins were made of bronze and only occasionally of iron, later to be replaced by brooches used as clothes fastenings. From the fifth century BC such brooches became widespread, with early continental La Tene diversifying into a series of insular types. At the hillfort of Twyn-y-Gaer, for example, iron La Tene brooches have been found similar in design to brooches from Croft Ambrey. Penannular brooches, rings, bracelets and beads have also been found. In addition to iron and bronze a variety of other materials were used: clay for pottery, loom weights, spindle-whorls and sling-shots; stone for quernstones and whetstones; bone for weaving combs and needles; and wood for houses, fences and trackways.

To kill or not to kill: Symbolic Warfare

Celtic society seems to have been dominated by a warrior ethic which sustained a social system bound up in the mythology of heroism and a cult of head-hunting. Individual prestige accrued from success in 'the fight', which, prior to the Roman conquest, would generally have taken the form of small scale confrontations between neighbouring clans. As the archaeologist Stuart Piggott has observed: 'Within this framework of warfare, conducted on a petty scale ... fit the practices of individual combat, ritual nakedness in battle, head-hunting, battle-cries and chants, and the rest of the excitements dear to the simple heart of the hero,' (Piggott, 1975, 40). Piggott's mention of head-hunting highlights a potent aspect of body-symbolism in Celtic society. The human head seems to have been a taboo object treated with a mixture of fear and reverence. In Polynesian society a man's head was the seat of his mana, a concept which signified both the ritual status of the individual and his soul or life-force. Similar beliefs are apparent among the Celts.

Potential evidence that head-hunting formed part of the Celtic raid was revealed at Bredon Hill in Worcestershire, where a row of six skulls was found in a way which suggested they had been displayed above a gateway close to where more than 60 people had been slaughtered. However, this seems to have been an exceptional incident, and was probably the work of the Romans as a warning to others. Indeed, warfare may well have been largely symbolic at this time, as with the medieval jousting tournament between champions. In the Central Highlands of Papua New Guinea opposing sides in any conflict set out to maim rather than to kill so that tribal numbers were not depleted. A number of hunter-gatherer rock paintings from the Spanish Levant (the east coast of Spain from Barcelona to Cadiz) and North Africa (the Tassili-n-Ajjer massif in southern Algeria) reveal a similar story. Many frescoes portray warring archers with elaborate head-dresses in pitched battle. However, the artist does not appear to show any dead or wounded warriors. Indeed, on a number of panels he or she suggests gladiatorial combat and execution were the main mechanisms for solving disputes. More recently, in the Trobriand Islands, west of Papua New Guinea, nineteenth century missionaries introduced 'Trobriand cricket' as a means of settling such disputes, and the game is still used in this way today. Again, among contemporary football fans similar formalised rituals have been observed. 'Fights' are 'more matters of the display of the signs, marks and instruments of aggression than they are of actual bodily encounters' (Harré, 1993, 214). The latter are said to be rare, and a successful fight is one which results in the enemy backing down. Forcing retreat in this way enhances the reputation of the 'victor'. Similarly, among the Celts there may well have been something of a discrepancy between the ideals of warring and the reality of conflict, the latter amounting to no more than exhibitionism and posturing on the part of a few prominent individuals.

This line of argument obviously presents problems for the conventional interpretation of hillforts as defensive works, and the traditional characterisation of Celts as a bloodthirsty and warlike people. It may only have been during the Roman invasion that mass slaughter occurred.

In addition to the ideal of warfare, that of cattle-raiding was also an important dynamic of Celtic society. It has been said of this society that '... cattle-raiding, and tales about this pastime, would have a high priority' (Ross, 1967, 39)—at least in those regions, such as parts of Monmouthshire, where pastoralism was practised. Cattle not only possessed symbolic value but constituted a significant form of wealth, and to deprive a person of his herds would have been to weaken his status and augment one's own. Indeed, some hillforts may have served in part as secure cattle pens. The early Irish text, the *Tain Bo Cuailgne* or the Cattle Raid of Cooley, and which belongs to the Ulster Cycle, is believed to reflect an oral tradition which predates the work's eventual literary form by centuries. Scholars have pointed out similarities between the world of the *Tain* and the Iron Age culture of Britain, and that of Gaulish society as seen through the eyes of Classical writers. Cattle-raiding was one of these common features. Beheading and chariot-fighting, boastfulness and warrior courage were others.

Monmouthshire—a tribal homeland?
With the Roman invasion the warrior ethic was vented against a new and powerful foe in a collective effort to preserve what would have been perceived as an age-old social system, bound up in myths

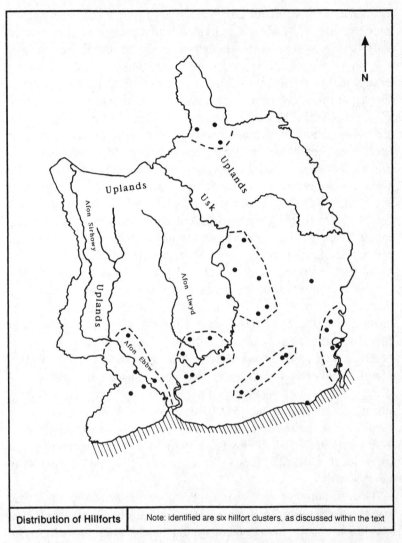

| Distribution of Hillforts | Note: identified are six hillfort clusters. as discussed within the text |

about the past. Local disputes would have been buried as tribes and confederacies surged into existence, the landscape crystallising into the mosaic of large territories described by foreign observers.

When the Romans extended their imperial ambitions into north-west Europe, they encountered a host of what they considered barbaric peoples, among the most ferocious of whom, it seems, were the Silures of South Wales. We can safely assume the descriptions which the Romans have bequeathed us were coloured by their own prejudices. Moreover, individual commanders would undoubtedly have exaggerated the strength of their foe in order to enhance their own military prestige. But given this inevitable bias, can we accept the basic picture of large contiguous tribal groupings within Britain at this time? We suggest that the invasion period was a time of unprecedented threat to communities living in South Wales, and that this period of profound disruption called for a much more inclusive form of social organisation than tradition dictated. The conquest thus stimulated the formation of vast tribal domains as a response to invasion or domination by a state-organised society as one definition of the tribal form of social organisation has it (Fried, 1975). Prior to this 'national emergency' the picture is unclear. Hogg underlines the need for caution when he says 'tribal locations are seldom known before the Roman period, and their boundaries usually have an uncertainty of 30 or 40km at least,' (Hogg, 1975, 39). We suggest that South Wales would probably have appeared as a mosaic of much smaller clan territories, each based upon one or several hillforts. The Roman invasion would have overridden these local loyalties and inter-clan boundaries—probably landscape features such as rivers—and helped to strengthen a larger 'Celtic' identity. In such a crisis, leaders of extraordinary qualities, such as Caratacos, would have emerged to weld clans together in probably uneasy alliance. Had the invasion never occurred, there would have been little scope for him, and others like him, to display their leadership qualities, and these people may well have remained small-time local chieftains engaged in petty tit-for-tat rivalry with neighbours.

This is not to say, however, that before the conquest Celtic society was static. To a large extent social change in the region would have been the result of gradual indigenous processes. But the influence of the Mediterranean world should not be underestimated. This may have begun to impinge upon these societies long before the Romans marched north. As has been pointed out for American Indian culture, European contact 'had begun to transform the native cultures of North America long before any significant amount of information was recorded about them. These changes altered societies hundreds of miles inland from the frontiers of actual European settlement and affected every aspect of Indian life.' (Trigger, 1978, 6).

The stamp of authority—hillforts and the landscape

Hillforts are generally thought to be an Iron Age phenomenon, yet a tradition of hilltop settlement can be traced back as far as the Neolithic (though Neolithic people avoided the highest mountain tops). It is true, however, that there was a rash of hillfort-building in Britain after about 750 BC, though many of the hillforts of Monmouthshire appear to have been constructed quite late in the Iron Age period. They are also rather small compared with the hillforts of the Welsh Marches, an observation which may suggest differences in social organisation between the two areas.

In total there are some 43 hillforts and up to 15 settlements and enclosures. The majority of Iron Age sites form a network along the rivers and large valleys of central Monmouthshire, with notable clustering close to the mouths of the rivers Usk and Wye. Larger monuments are strategically sited on the major meanders of both rivers, dominating the rich alluvial flood plains. The vast majority of hillforts in Monmouthshire enclose an area under 1.2 hectares. There are only six sites which exceed 2 hectares, and only two of these possess complex defences using a multivallate system. This would suggest the population density per hillfort area, whether permanent or temporary settlement is proposed, was relatively small—possibly between one and five extended families. Hillfort-building may often have been a co-operative venture, drawing in neighbouring families from the surrounding farmsteads. Such co-operation would have been an effective prelude to the formation of larger social entities at the time of the Roman invasion of Wales.

A central place model applied to nine marches hillforts has revealed the possible extent of these co-operative networks. The hillforts studied appear to have been in use between 600 BC and 200 BC, and the model suggested each had a catchment area extending about 5km beyond the immediate surroundings of the site. Within these catchments, as yet poorly recognized settlements were believed to have provisioned the hillforts (Gent & Dean, 1986, 30). They may also have provided labour for the construction of these sites. Similar work needs to be carried out in Monmouthshire to establish whether such a conclusion is valid here, although central place theory, which was developed for use in economic geography, has had its share of critics in the archaeological world and many would question the results.

A general trend in hillfort design concerns the elaboration of entrances. In Neolithic tomb architecture—and also perhaps Bronze Age stone circles—the entrance or doorway attained a special significance as the liminal, or transitional zone between two wholly different spaces—sacred and secular—and the performance of rituals in the entrance and forecourt area seems to have been an important aspect of tomb use. There is no suggestion that hillforts had a principally funerary or ritual function, although some may have contained shrines. Hogg, for example, believed Maiden Castle in Dorset had a substantial 'sacred centre' which persisted from the construction of the hillfort to the end of the Roman period. Yet the resurgence of interest in the entrance and the construction of increasingly monumental gateways with inturned entrances at some hillforts suggests a heightened concern with the interior as a special-status space within the local community, to which access had to be signified and perhaps restricted. It has been suggested that such portals act like valves—'passage out is easier than passage in, so that while not all who aspire are admitted, all who have been admitted eventually come out' (Harré, 1993, 154). Harré further observes that there is often 'a ceremonial performance' involved in achieving entry to a public building, while 'a mere valedictory nod' is sufficient on leaving the enclosed area. The same could be said of the medieval city, with its elaborate gates and symbolic separation of the internal walled area (the political and cultural) and the surrounding countryside (the natural and rustic).

As A.H.A. Hogg has observed, there was nothing startlingly new in the technology of hillfort construction—many of the techniques had been used two millennia before by the builders of Neolithic monuments (Hogg, 1975, 58). It is more likely to have been the ideas associated with hillforts rather than the technology involved in their construction that were imported into Monmouthshire. As Stanford, who excavated several hillforts in the Marches, observes, '... prehistoric communities often acquired objects and ideas from afar and communications seem to have been comparatively efficient' (Stanford, 1991, 43). The Iron Age societies of South Wales were not insulated from outside influences.

A modernist icon, the Brynmawr rubber factory, offers a latter-day example of the deliberate importation of 'foreign' architectural ideas into Monmouthshire, ideas which were intended to transform the environment of the area by stimulating a post-war industrial resurgence. The factory was designed between 1946 and 1951, following negotiations between the South Wales and Monmouthshire Trading Estate and Enfield Cables Ltd. The resulting structure incorporated architectural principles and aesthetics which were then circulating throughout Europe. Although the building was comprised of simple structural components, the overall effect was one of spatial complexity. The same could be said of many hillforts. Although further excavation is needed to elucidate the internal spatial arrangements, and the often poor survival of evidence is always a problem, those Marches hillforts excavated by Stanford do seem to indicate a sophisticated arrangement of space. Admired by Frank Lloyd Wright and eulogised as 'one of the most extraordinary and romantic projects in the history of British architecture', Brynmawr possessed a profound affinity with its landscape and even seemed to replicate the bleak undulating moorland in which it was set, 'the vaults of the concrete shell roof ... echoing the shapes of the rolling mountains' (Perry, 1994, 42). The harmony of building and landscape created an emotive effect, and, while the functionalism of the design was emphasised by the architects, the Brynmawr rubber factory above all symbolised the economic regeneration of an area hit by industrial decline. The project enabled local planners to link Monmouthshire to the rest of Europe and the wider ideology of modernism, with its promise of a brave new future. The fairly rapid collapse of this ideology has left the factory derelict, one disused monument among many scattered across the landscape, its status usurped by a new electronics factory embodying a new aesthetic. As the first post-war building to be listed, it now no longer symbolises hope for the future, rather it embodies a set of values concerned with preserving the past and consolidating a history—a social history of Monmouthshire.

Industrial decline is clearly a phenomenon of more recent times, but some have linked the appearance of hillforts with other 'environmental' factors such as climatic deterioration and population increase. It has been said that these factors caused social instability and conflict, giving rise to the need for elaborate defensive works. However, interpreting hillforts as a simple response to these kinds of stimuli may conceal a more complex situation in which, as in the above example, symbolism and the manipulation of ideas played a leading role. A prestigious project such as Brynmawr which CADW has described as a modern factory complex of worldwide significance conferred status on an area which in the eyes of neighbouring regions across the border was condemned as 'poor' or 'deprived'. Imported ideas were thus used to strengthen local identity and improve the status of local people, showing them able to compete socially with their neighbours.

The integration of an Iron Age landscape

The Severn Estuary mudflats have recently revealed a unique 1.4km fragment of Iron Age landscape—a specialised estuarine settlement, possibly only occupied for a relatively brief period. The site, at Goldcliff, comprised a complex of substantial rectangular wooden buildings and trackways, and may have been occupied by a fishing community. Some of the preserved wooden structures have been interpreted as fish traps, while the remains of boats discovered nearby suggest this may also have served as a ferry point across the estuary. Due to its possible seasonal or temporary use, Goldcliff may not have been an important settlement and its relationship to the hillforts is obscure. The nearest is Wilcrick Hill, some twelve kilometres north-east, further than the more usual five kilometres radius of 'control', increasing the probability that the site was only used on a temporary basis. It should be noted, however, that the settlement, albeit temporary or seasonal, would have been modelled on similar house structures elsewhere. The plan of buildings 1 and 2 (see page 95) may represent more than just a mundane layout.

To the east and west of Goldcliff, a series of strategically placed promontory hillforts line the northern shores of the Bristol Channel. It would appear that they may have formed a line of outposts possibly serving as beacon stations for incoming water traffic as well as political meeting places. Each fort has a similar layout with defences on three sides, with the southern flank protected by cliffs. Each internal enclosure is positioned so as to visually command the channel approaches.

Away from the coast the picture is one dominated by hillforts. But in addition to these there are a number of 'farmsteads', each comprising one or more houses grouped together with storage facilities in the form of pits and granaries. The best known Iron Age farmstead is that of Little Woodbury, in Wiltshire (Bersu, 1940). This consisted of a central round house surrounded by granaries and pits and enclosed by a palisade and ditch. Recently, revised dating has indicated that this settlement was in use from the sixth century BC, whilst aerial survey has revealed fairly dense activity close to the site. A multi-phase Iron Age farmstead excavated at Whitton, in south Glamorgan, revealed a similar pattern of round houses within a palisade. In Monmouthshire, a number of farmsteads have been identified. The distribution of these to some extent reflects the varying intensity of research in the county. Tradition states that Tregare Church was built within a British camp, and investigations reported in *Archaeology in Wales* (No. 29, 1989) revealed a curving earth bank and ditch concealed beneath a hedge in an adjacent field to the north. This feature swings around to the south-west before ending just short of the Dingestow to Bryngwyn road. The site is located within a slightly undulating landscape about 10km from the hillfort of Coed y Bwynydd. A similar landscape setting is evident at Bryngwyn (SO 391 079) 3km to the south-west. Here, a comparable farmstead was investigated by Judy Leslie in 1962. The pottery discovered on the site was late, dating to the second and third centuries AD. The farmstead, however, is believed to date from the pre-Roman period, and given its proximity to Coed y Bwynydd it may well have served as a satellite settlement. A possible fenced farmstead complex at Trostrey (SO 360 043) lies 2.5km west of Llancayo close to a bend in the River Usk. The palisade may have been closed by a portable hurdle gate (*Archaeology in Wales* No. 34, 1994). Postholes of round houses were discovered at the site and pottery from one of these has been dated to the fourth century BC. Further examples of Iron Age pottery from a linear firepit have been compared with types discovered at Magor Pill on the Severn

Estuary. At Home Farm, Cwm y Gwcw, Llanhennock Fawr (ST 362 931) an apparently multi-phase complex comprised field boundaries and round houses. The latter lay within a sub-circular ditched enclosure with gateway—indicated by massive post pits to the north-east. It has been suggested by the Trostrey Excavation Group that the huts were not all in use at the same time (*Archaeology in Wales* No.32, 1992).

These farmsteads were probably home to extended families, the basic social units of a broadly mixed farming economy. Other classes of settlement were seasonal, such as Goldcliff, while some may have had a specialised function. For example, the Roman name for Abergavenny, *Gobannium*, means 'place of the iron worker' and excavations in Flannel Street have yielded Iron Age pottery sherds, indicating that a settlement of this date existed on the site. It is believed that here a specialised iron-working community exploited metal ores from around Pwll-du. All of these settlements may have been subservient to local hillforts, with products from surrounding territories being channelled inwards to these central places for storage and redistribution.

Symbolism or function: the role of the hillfort

Against a straightforward interpretation of hillforts as permanent settlements, it has been frequently argued that many lack the water supplies necessary for continuous occupation. Perhaps hillforts were used only periodically for seasonal 'fairs' or as temporary refuges in times of crisis. Many questions remain unanswered. Indeed, there may not be a single answer; hillforts may have served a variety of functions. Llanmelin, for example, has been identified as the tribal capital of the Silures before they were subjugated by the Romans and moved to the new settlement of Caerwent, some 3km away. Twyn-y-Gaer, in the north of the county where pastoral farming may have been more important, has been interpreted as a corral, at least in its earliest phases. Sudbrook, on the Severn Estuary, seems to have been a late hillfort, possibly designed to 'guard' an important Bristol Channel crossing between Aust and Portskewett.

These interpretations suggest hillfort-builders used a limited repertoire of basic architectural forms to serve a variety of purposes: political, economic and strategic. Moreover, we have to consider the possibility that the function of hillforts changed over time, perhaps as society became more complex during the period leading up to the expansion of Rome. Generally, the trend is from simple to elaborate ramparts and entrances. Hillforts also tend to increase in size, although some—notably Twyn-y-Gaer—appear to have contracted in later periods. In parts of southern Britain some hillforts were abandoned altogether, while others continued to evolve towards the status of true 'central places', possibly serving expanded territories as storage, administrative and craft production centres. In Monmouthshire, however, there seems to be little evidence for the emergence of this kind of dominance.

Underlying each of these interpretations is the belief that hillforts assumed the form they did for reasons of defence. The political leaders of a community needed to be protected from attack, cattle needed to be safeguarded from the predations of raiding parties and coastal stations had to be strong enough to repel unwelcome landings. We would prefer to look beyond this functional interpretation, however, to the ideas which hillforts may have embodied. After all, as has been observed 'it is precisely the *idea* of what forms may most appropriately be selected which creates the architecture of a particular age,' (Collins, 1965, 16).

In this book we have attempted to veer away from the popular conception of hillforts as defensive works which arose during times of stress, suggesting instead that the value of their ramparts, ditches and monumental gateways was to a large extent symbolic—that these man-made features, which involved a remodelling of the landscape, created a rhetoric of forms that was widely adopted in temperate Europe at this time to express certain common cultural values linked to the warrior ideal. Indeed, it may only have been during the 'national emergency' of the Roman invasion that hillforts served any real military-strategic need. Earlier, these prominent defences, social and political statements, would have signified the special status of hillforts as central places and territorial focal points within local communities. We would further argue that the visibility of hillforts was enhanced by landscape positioning. Of course, the siting of hillforts on high ground is usually interpreted as a defensive measure. However, it could be argued that these locations were chosen because intervisibility between neighbouring hillforts was an important component of territory-formation and maintenance. Thus, hillfort communities within sight of each other would have shared a common socio-political identity.

Goldcliff

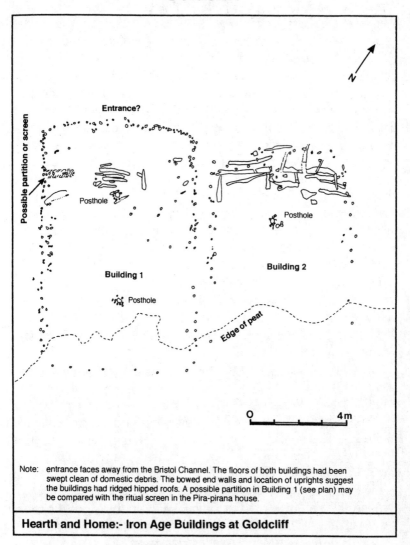

Hearth and Home:- Iron Age Buildings at Goldcliff

Nothing to see
Location: On the Severn Estuary, to the east
of the mouth of the Usk (ST 362 820)

Possibly a short-lived and specialised fishing site comprising the remains of substantial rectangular buildings, the Goldcliff site on the Severn Estuary Levels was revealed in 1990 following gales and high tides. A total of eight buildings were discovered on a peat shelf during the course of several seasons' work. These were constructed of vertical posts bearing the marks of iron axes. Timbers from the excavation, which was carried out under the auspices of St David's University College at Lampeter, have been conserved at Newport Museum. Interestingly, the interiors were devoid of hearths and other evidence of domestic occupation. Sections of Iron Age wooden trackways were also found nearby.

A series of radiocarbon dates was recorded indicating that the site dates from the second century BC. Building 1 measured 5.6m by 8.4m with a possible entrance at the north-western end measuring 0.6m wide. Traces of wattle walling were found, and there was a well-preserved floor in the north-west corner. This was covered by a layer of reeds. Central posts may have supported a ridged hipped roof and internal partitions divided the building in half. Only one bone was discovered inside the building, but a bone and antler scatter was found around the entrance. The entrance to the buildings is orientated north-west, away from the prevailing winds that funnel up the Bristol Channel.

The adjacent building to the east and parallel to building 1 was separated from it by a 0.5m wide alley. This slightly smaller second building measured 5.2m by 7.4m and had a possible entrance measuring 0.9m wide. There were again traces of flooring but no internal partitions. The remains of other rectangular buildings were later discovered. A double row of stakes running 33m to the north may have been contemporary with the buildings or a later fish trap. All of the buildings were subject to flooding by the sea while in use.

A brushwood trackway was found 100m north-east of the excavated buildings. The track varied in width from 0.5m to 1.35m and covered a distance of 44m. Another trackway, 145m to the east of the brushwood example, was of different construction. A possible length of track leading to one of the rectangular structures consisted of brushwood laid between posts and is regarded as notable among the many trackways of prehistoric Europe. The remains of boats were also discovered nearby. It has been suggested that the lack of artefacts and hearths, plus the evidence for flooding, suggests activity at the site was temporary and seasonal, perhaps associated with grazing or other utilisation of estuarine resources. Animal hoof prints were discovered outside building 8. However, according to Dr Martin Bell, who was involved with the project, an alternative ritual or symbolic use has also to be considered (Bell, Archaeology in Wales No. 31, 1991).

A possible symbolic interpretation of the Goldcliff complex may be derived from the South American research of the anthropologist Stephen Hugh-Jones. He noted that many sedentary societies place symbolic value on entrance location. Focusing upon the Pira-parana long house, Hugh-Jones (1979) observed that men and women have different doorways and that arrangements within the house are such that men's and women's spaces are physically separated by a screen. The metaphor is that of the human body. The women's entrance is regarded as an opening through which faeces, or dirt, are discharged, whilst the men's door allows speech and breath, as well as food, to enter the house (see the accompanying plan). Inside, food and speech circulate around the body, whilst dirt is

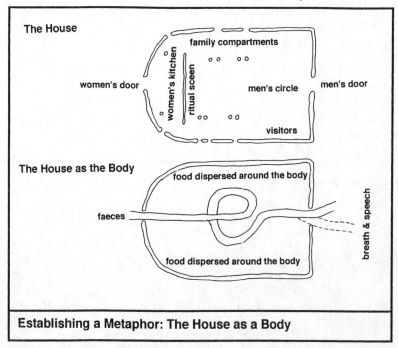

Establishing a Metaphor: The House as a Body

expelled via the women's door. The body is constantly purged so that it remains healthy and the occupants prosper. Again, among gypsies, there is a rigid separation of clean and dirty space, dividing the immediate domestic area from the rest of the encampment. In this way, the hearth and home remains a source of pride for the owner.

When excavated, the buildings at Goldcliff revealed very little internal domestic debris—they had apparently been swept clean—while a scatter of bones was found around the entrance. Without proposing a direct analogy between the Pira-parana long house or the gypsy encampment and the buildings at Goldcliff, the use of ethnography does provide a fresh approach to the archaeological evidence, raising questions of interpretation that might not otherwise be asked.

Bulwarks Camp

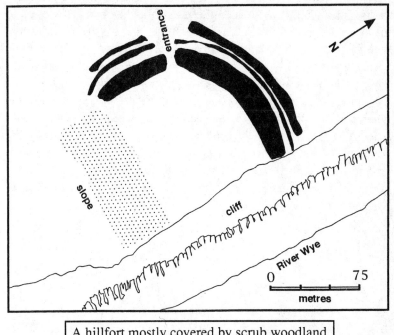

A hillfort mostly covered by scrub woodland
Location: In the south of Chepstow,
above the Wye (ST 538 927)
Access: Can be reached by public footpath
from the centre of the town

This hillfort stands on a promontory overlooking the River Severn within the town of Chepstow. From Chepstow Castle, head south towards the area of the town known as Bulwark. The hillfort is clearly signposted halfway up the hill.

Alternatively, there is a footpath that passes the hillfort, running from the old port walls at Hardwick in the centre of Chepstow to Thornwell. The authors recommend walking this path as it takes in the ancient walls, the hillfort and Thornwell chambered tomb (see separate entry), and the walk can be extended to the north to take in the castle.

The eastern flank occupies cliffs overlooking the River Wye, tidal at this point, and has dominant views of the Wye Gorge to the north and south. On the southern portion of the hillfort little remains of the defences. Here the hillfort stands above a treacherous slope plunging down to the mouth of the river. However, to the west and north the defences comprise a triple bank and ditch, with an open entrance and possible causeway. Andrews Downman, surveying the monument in 1911, recognised that the outer two banks were separated by a raised ditch running parallel with them. The inner ditch appeared to be below ground level, suggesting the innermost rampart is by far the largest and would have been built first. At present, both the hillfort and the surrounding area are covered by dense scrub woodland. However, the entrance and ramparts to the north and south can be clearly seen. Bulwarks Camp is one of only a handful of larger hillforts (i.e. more than 0.2ha) within the county.

Pen-Twyn Hillfort

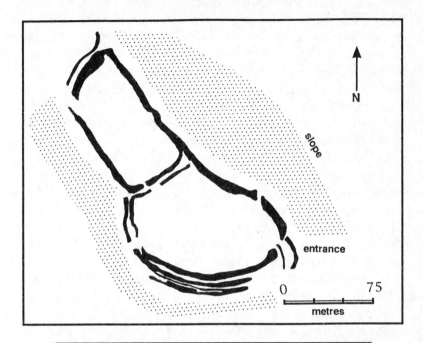

A hillfort with double bank and ditch with fine views
Location: 8km north of Abergavenny (SO 321 230)
Access: The hillside is criss-crossed with public paths

From Abergavenny proceed north towards Hereford along the A465 to the village of Llanvihangel Crucorney. Take the first left signposted 'Llanthony Priory'. Keeping left at the first junction, follow the road for approximately 2.5km and take the right turn past the Queen's Head. Follow the road as far as a crossroads, 1km beyond the turn. Take the left turning up a steep incline past Lower Pentwyn. The hillfort is clearly visible on a south-east facing ridge to the right.

Less is known about Pen-Twyn (332m above sea level) than its neighbour Twyn-y-Gaer. Both are positioned along the southern edge of the Black Mountains, sites which command panoramic views of the surrounding landscape. Like Twyn-y-Gaer, Pen-Twyn appears to be a multi-phase structure. A cross bank and ditch divides the enclosure in two and may once have formed its boundary on the southern side. The larger area to the south may be a later addition, possibly—as at Twyn-y-Gaer—originally serving as an annexe. This annexe may have been enclosed by a fence before the construction of an earthen rampart incorporated it within the hillfort. This rampart is now constructed of a double bank and ditch, an arrangement also demonstrated at Twyn-y-Gaer. An elaborate inturned entrance at the south-east corner of the southern enclosure ensured the approach to the hillfort was closely controlled, the gate looking over the point at which the Afon Honddu flows into the River Monnow. In turn, the entrance at Twyn-y-Gaer faces east and also overlooks the river, which may have acted as a boundary between the territories of the hillforts. It is not suggested that the two hillforts were in conflict, rather that in each case there was the social and political recognition of a neighbour. Interestingly, approximately 5km south of Pen-Twyn and 5.5km south-east of Twyn-y-Gaer stands Llanddewi Sgyrrid (SO 331 183). This hillfort appears to share a similar relationship to the river as its more northerly neighbours, suggesting that the river may again have formed the boundary between recognized territories.

Twyn-y-Gaer

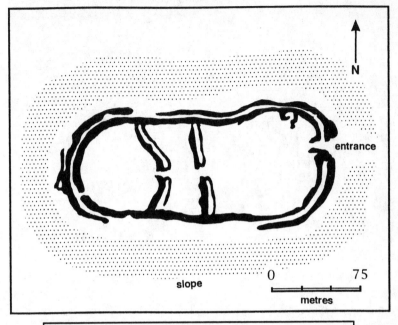

N

entrance

slope

0   75

metres

Hillfort with only low banks and ditches remaining,
but with wide views
Location: 7km north of Abergavenny (SO 294 219)
Access: Footpaths lead up from the road below

From Abergavenny proceed north towards Hereford along the A465
to the village of Llanvihangel Crucorney. Take the first left signposted 'Llanthony Priory'. Follow the road around to the left for
about 2.5km as far as the Queen's Head. Take a left turn and follow
the track past the turning for Gaer Farm. Footpaths lead south from
this road to the impressive hillfort, which is clearly visible from the
road. (The public right-of-way is the path towards the western end
of the hill, which leaves the road opposite the end of the woodland.)

Twyn-y-Gaer, which stands 550m above sea level, is the most
intensively investigated of the three hillforts 'guarding' the
southern extent of the Black Mountains. (See also Pen-Twyn. The
third fort, Crug Hywel, lies in Powys). There is a further hillfort to
the south-east on the Skirrid (SO 331 183). Some have argued that

it was only during later phases that the site came under the influence of the Silures, as the 'tribe' extended its power northwards (Probert, 1976, 118). This suggestion was based upon changes in gateway design and pottery styles. Evidence for the earlier periods reveals affinities with hillforts of the central Marches, such as Croft Ambrey and Midsummer Hill in Herefordshire. But from about the third century BC, Twyn-y-Gaer seems to have been drawn within the cultural ambit of the southern Monmouthshire hillforts, yielding pottery similar to types found at Llanmelin and Sudbrook. We would argue, however, that prior to the Roman invasion social and political territories were much smaller than these observations would suggest, and that there seems to be little justification for linking such broad changes in material culture with patterns of 'tribal' expansion or political domination.

The ramparts at Twyn-y-Gaer enclose a 1.8ha hilltop overlooking the Vale of Ewyas and the Afon Honddu valley, within the transitional zone between uplands and lowlands. The interior of the hillfort is divided into three parts: the western portion, which has an area of around 0.5ha; a central area of 0.3ha and the larger eastern enclosure of roughly 0.9ha. It appears the eastern section was originally a fenced enclosure, which may have been used for corralling livestock. The fence was of birch and had been renewed eight times before the construction of an earthen rampart brought the so-called 'annexe' within the main body of the hillfort. A calibrated radiocarbon date of 392 BC has been established for the final fence-phase, and Probert estimates that the first fence was built around 470 BC (Probert, 116). The hillfort was reduced in size to the 0.5ha western part during its final use.

As Probert points out, 'compared with the Herefordshire forts, the earthworks are diminutive, rarely standing more then a metre high above the present ground surface inside' (Probert, 1977, 107). Stone revetments, he said, gave the ramparts additional substance. Particular attention seems to have been lavished on the eastern entrance, where a stone-revetted passageway, a partially-enclosed space, led up to the gates. Anyone approaching the hillfort would have been struck by the visually impressive facade formed by the revetment. The gateway itself may have had a distinct threshold, a timber baulk set in a transverse slot, which would have defined the transitional point at the end of the controlled approach through the passageway where one crossed from the outside world into the interior of the hillfort. The visual impact of the entrance area would have been increased by the later addition of a stone rampart walkway. Thresholds indicated by gateway slots have also been identified at the Herefordshire hillforts of Croft Ambrey and Midsummer Hill. Unlike the apparently dense pattern of structures found within the hillforts of the central Marches, however, the interior of Twyn-y-Gaer revealed only meagre structural traces of round houses, which Stanford believed were probably turf-walled.

Most of the finds discovered during excavations came from the east gate area. Pottery has not been definitely identified in the earliest period, although a sherd bearing fingernail decoration may date from this phase. During the middle phase, examples of Malvern stamped ware were found, as were iron La Tene brooches of similar design to examples found at Croft Ambrey. Later pottery has been linked to sites in southern Monmouthshire and interpreted as evidence of a shift in political and cultural orientation at this time. A selection of tools, a few curved knives and a broken spear-head were also found, together with quernstones and traces of metalworking.

Llancayo Camp

An impressive hillfort with triple banks and ditches
Location: 3km north of Usk (SO 378 038)
Access: In CADW guardianship and can be viewed from a track
which passes close by

From Usk take the B4598 and head along this road for 3km. Take
the first right signposted 'Llancayo'. Follow this road for approximately 2km towards the village of Gwehelog. Before the village
there is a track and footpath which follows the eastern side of
Llancaeo Hill. Park near here and walk along this track for roughly
700m. On the right hand side, and clearly visible, are the outer
defences of this impressive hillfort.

On the north-east ridge of Llancaeo Hill, this lightly-wooded hillfort commands outstanding views in all directions. The hill falls
away dramatically to the west, east and north. On the south side
there is a very interesting entrance complex. Outworks consisting of
three banks and ditches are located beyond the towering main
defences. It appears these were purposely laid out so as to impede
direct access to the southern entrance. This device could be interpreted as a means of strengthening that part of the hillfort which

was weakest defensively. However, the outworks could have been designed purely to create a visual impact. Inside the main southern rampart, a linear depression may be the result of quarrying to provide earth for the bank. To the west of the interior are features which could also be quarries, or possibly wells. Investigations within the central area of the hillfort during tree-planting produced two worn lower stones belonging to rotary querns, probably of the 'beehive' type.

The hillfort not only commands the small plateau of Llancaeo Hill but also has extensive views over the fertile plains of the Usk Valley to the south-west. Surprisingly, beyond the Usk there is no evidence of Iron Age activity, suggesting that, politically, the influence of the hillfort may have extended towards lands south and west of the Usk Valley. To the east, the hillforts of Great House and Gaer-fawr are strategically placed and almost equidistant between two major river courses flowing south-west into the Usk—Pill Brook and Olway Brook. Once again, it is suggested that these natural features acted as socio-political boundaries between the three hillforts. To the north, approximately 6km away, is Coed y Bwynydd. This hillfort occupies a similarly dominant position over the Usk Valley.

Coed y Bwynydd Camp

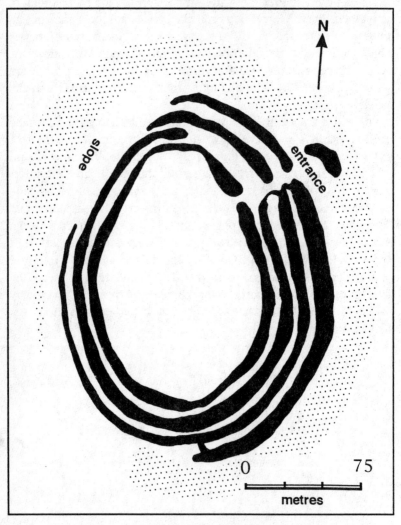

One of the finest hillforts of Monmouthshire,
with triple banks and ditches
Location: 5km west of Raglan (SO 366 068)
Access: Owned by the National Trust with free access

From the Raglan roundabout on the A40, take the northern exit and follow the road parallel with the A40 through Wern-y-cwrt. Continue for approximately 4km from the roundabout to a cross-roads. Take the left turning signposted 'Bettws Newydd'. Head along this road for roughly 2.5km. Coed y Bwynydd hillfort is clearly visible on top of Clytha Hill to the right.

In 1914, the hillfort was said to be 'much overgrown with trees and underwood and is not easily examined,' (Andrews Downman, 1916, 8). However, by April 1996, the ramparts and enclosure had been cleared of scrub vegetation.

Now owned by the National Trust, Coed y Bwynydd Camp, is one of the finest 'model' hillforts in Monmouthshire. The defences consist of a triple bank and ditch complex on the northern, eastern and southern sides. To the west, the hillfort is defended by, possibly, a single bank but mainly the steep slope of Clytha Hill. The multivallate system of defences begins on the north side of the hillfort, merging into the hillside on the west. On the north-east side is evidence of revetment material and an entrance cutting straight through the ramparts. The area beyond the camp itself is covered by deciduous woodland and this obscures the view of the Usk Valley and the mountains to the west. However, Coed y Bwynydd, like Llancayo Camp, was sited so as to be seen. Its size is similar to the majority of hillforts in Monmouthshire: approximately 0.3 ha. Two radiocarbon dates of around 400 BC have been obtained from timber belonging to a round house, one of four excavated on the site.

Great House Camp

High bank and ditch
Location: 6km north-east of Usk (SO 432 033)
Access: Visible from a minor lane that cuts
through the outer defences

From Usk proceed east along the A472 towards the A449 Newport to Monmouth road. Before reaching this, turn left onto the B4235 towards Llangwm. Approximately 1km beyond the A449, bear left onto a country lane towards the hamlet of Pen-y-clawdd. After about 3.4km, take a right turn signposted 'Llansoy'. The hillfort is located 0.8km along this road, the outer defences on the north-eastern side being cut by the road.

The position of Great House Camp, standing in undulating landscape 90m above sea level, is such that it is equidistant from Gaerfawr and Llancayo Camps. Furthermore, all three hillforts are divided by the valleys of the Olway Brook and Pill Brook. Again we suggest these natural landscape features act as political-territorial boundaries. Great House Camp is surrounded by a roughly circular triple bank and ditch system and is on a small hillock. Andrews Downman, when surveying the site in 1914, identified a simple entrance to the south.

Sudbrook Camp

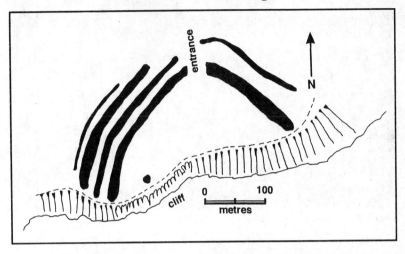

> Hillfort with ramparts reaching over 5 metres high
> Location: To the south of Portskewett
> on the Severn Estuary (ST 505 873)
> Access: A public footpath runs across the site

To the east of the church in Portskewett, take the road south, crossing one railway line and then following another till the Severn Estuary is immediately ahead. The hillfort is located behind a line of railway buildings to the south and a footpath links an old church with the fort along the edge of the Gwent Levels.

Sudbrook Camp is one of the Gwent Levels' promontory hill-forts. To the north-east of the hillfort and close to its outer ramparts is the Severn Tunnel. It stands on cliffs 17m above the Bristol Channel and has been linked with a possible crossing point over the estuary. It has been interpreted as a trading post which was almost certainly larger than it appears today (1.4ha), for part has probably been destroyed by coastal erosion. This suggestion was confirmed, in January, 1911, by Andrews Downman. William Camden, the antiquarian, described its layout as a bow, the cliff representing the string. The ramparts reach a height of 5.2m and the defences consist of three ditches and an internal quarry ditch extending in total for

58m. On the western side, a small bank runs through the middle of what was possibly a much deeper and steeply-inclined ditch.

Minor excavations in 1934-36 revealed that two V-shaped ditches between the ramparts on the north-west side of the main bank were built in four stages. On the inner scarp there were two steep-sloping revetments of uncoursed drystone walling. Two sub-rectangular ditches were identified inside the bank. Evidence from both ditches revealed occupation from the mid-second century BC to the mid-second century AD. The excavation also revealed evidence of use by the Romans. Finds included bones of oxen, pigs, sheep or goat, together with glass and iron. It may well have become a Roman supply depot.

Lodge Wood Camp

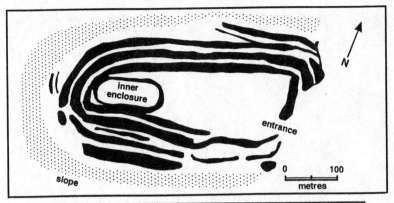

One of Monmouthshire's larger hillforts
Location: On the western edge of Caerleon (ST 323 913)
Access: Public footpaths lead through the fort
from the edge of the town

From the Roman museum in Caerleon, proceed north along the B4236 for about 0.2km. Just over the railway line, take the first left and follow the road to a hospital. Take a right turn in front of the hospital and follow this road northwards for about 100 metres. Lodge Wood Camp is sited on undulating pasture behind a single row of houses and in front of Lodge Wood itself.

The hillfort is located on a valley ridge overlooking Caerleon and once had a commanding position to the north and south. The foot of the ridge is flanked on the north, east and southern sides by the Afon Llwyd and the lower reaches of the Usk.

The first hillfort on this site comprised a single bank enclosing an area of around 0.5ha. In common with many hillforts it underwent subsequent elaboration.

Tredegar Fort

© GGAT

A hillfort later incorporated into eighteenth century
landscaping and a subsequent golf course
Location: On the western edge of Newport (ST 289 868)
Access: From the golf course

This hillfort stands, not in Tredegar, but in west Newport, between a housing estate and the M4 motorway. From junction 27 of the M4, head east along the B4591 into Newport. After the first roundabout, approximately 2km from junction 27, proceed toward Stow Park. Take the second right signposted 'Cemetery'. Head along this road for about 2.5km past the cemetery. The hillfort is clearly visible in open heathland on the left.

Sited on one of the highest points in the Newport area (90m above sea level), this fort is one of five strategically placed around the mouth of the River Usk and its tributaries. Similar to Lodge Wood, some 8km north-east, Tredegar Fort commands the approaches between the Usk, in the east, and the Ebbw, in the west. The Ebbw is equidistant between Rhiwderin Camp (ST 264 877) and Duffryn (ST 273 862). It would appear that all three hillforts west of Newport are placed so as to command strategic points on the Ebbw River, with the rivers acting as territorial boundaries.

The banks and ditches have over the recent past been much disturbed. Part of the inner enclosure has been destroyed by a golf tee and bunker. Furthermore, banks and ditches forming the outer enclosure have been partly destroyed by quarrying on the eastern side. Having said that, the hillfort appears to follow the contours of the hill and to be roughly circular. It comprises an inner enclosure with evenly spaced triple banks and ditches. To the south, and probably a later addition, is a crescent-shaped enclosure which may have served as a corral for stock and been integrated within the main body of the hillfort by a single bank and ditch.

The changing perception and utilisation of landscape is well illustrated at Tredegar Fort. Beginning as an Iron Age construction, it had, by the early eighteenth century become incorporated into an ornamental landscape. This was under the direction of the Morgan family of Tredegar House, some 1.8km to the south. From the top of the hill the owners were not only able to survey their lands, but, standing among the ramparts, to engender a romantic sense of history. The fort and the house are separated by the Ebbw River, which, rather than demarcating socio-political territories, as it may well have done during the Iron Age, then served to separate the new from the old.

From this phase of landscaping until Andrews Downman surveyed the fort in 1910, there appears to have been little activity. We may assume, therefore, that the only entrance approach to the fort was one which he identified to the south-east. This would make sense, given that the western slope of the hill is too steep to accommodate horse-drawn traffic, whereas the eastern side is gently sloping. Subsequently, however, the fort once again witnessed a change in landscape perception. No longer a statement on the landscape, it became more or less invisible, part of the inner enclosure being obliterated by a bunker and tee during the laying out of a golf course. Furthermore, banks and ditches forming the outer enclosure have been partly destroyed by quarrying on the eastern side. Today, the monument has been incorporated within a conception of landscape as heritage. In this landscape the old is privileged and legally protected from the encroachment of the new.

Llanmelin Wood Camps

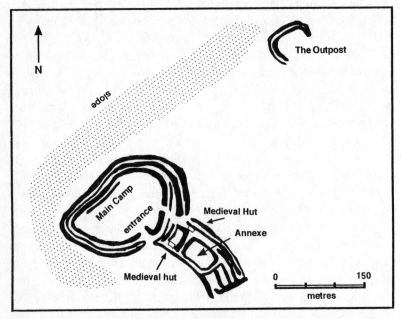

A hillfort with a series of enclosures
Location: 7km west of Chepstow (ST 461 925 & ST 463 928)
In the care of CADW and reached by footpaths

From the roundabout on the A466 on the north-western edge of Chepstow, take the B4235 towards Usk. Some 5.5km along the road, just before reaching Mynydd-bach, take a left turn signposted 'Shirenewton'. Drive through the village towards Llanvair Discoed. Approximately 1.5km from Shirenewton, and past woodland (Cuhere Wood), is a footpath sign on the left. Park near here and follow the footpath into the wood for 300m. The western hillfort defences are clearly visible.

Located on a south-facing ridge, this monument, the larger of two Llanmelin camps, is, nevertheless, one of Monmouthshire's smaller hillforts. It was excavated in 1930-32 by Nash-Williams, who considered it to have been built during the second century BC. The hillfort is, however, probably far older. Consisting of an oval enclosure of 1.2ha, Llanmelin also has an annexe to the south-east. Complex in form, the ground plan of this annexe indicates a series of rectangular features. Some are probably corralling enclosures and may be later additions constructed in response to an increase in population (Hogg, 1975). Others are medieval structures.

Annexes are not uncommon in this part of Britain and their use is still open to debate. However, we suggest they were built as corrals or trading-rings in response to an expanding Iron Age economy. Dyer in his *Prehistoric Sites of England and Wales* has hinted that the annexes resemble medieval fishponds. However, the location of the hillfort, high on a small escarpment overlooking the Caldicot Levels, suggests this use would have been impractical and uneconomic. Moreover, there is no substantial early medieval settlement close to the site.

The form of the hillfort is dictated by the hill on which it stands. The defences consist of a double rampart, ditch and counterscarp. Hogg argues the projection at the north-east is a vestige of the original earthworks—a single rampart. Between 140 and 170 BC, contemporary with a new wave of hillfort activity in Gloucestershire and Herefordshire, this was obliterated by a double ditch and bank, the inner rampart of which was built of a massive 5m thick drystone wall. The outer defence comprises debris from the original bank and ditch. Gateposts were installed at the inner end of an entrance passage. An asymmetrical ditch is located to the south-east, close to the later annexe feature.

Around 50 BC, a final construction phase resulted in the redesign and elaboration of the entrance. Elizabeth Whittle suggests this was carried out as a response to an 'increased threat of attack'. However we suggest this is more of a visual statement on the landscape. Doorways in our own society at least partially signify who and what one is. Likewise entrances to hillforts embodied political power and prestige.

An excavation carried out in 1991 to the east of the hillfort confirmed the existence of a trackway recognised by Nash-Williams in 1932, and which may have served as the approach road to the entrance.

Approximately 250m north-east of the main hillfort is an earthwork referred to as 'the Outpost'. Nothing is known about the relationship between the two. The Outpost could have served as a settlement area linked to the main camp, which may have been used for corralling, the exchange of stock and as a political meeting place. Constructed of a semi-circular double bank and ditch, the Outpost appears to be unprotected on its south-eastern flank. The entire complex was finally abandoned around 75 AD.

Finds from the fort are meagre, consisting of a few sherds of middle Iron Age date and some Roman and medieval material. The remains of red deer were also discovered. Antiquarians have suggested that Llanmelin may have been the capital of the Silures before they were moved to Caerwent, some 3km to the south. However, Hogg has cast doubt on the argument that Llanmelin was ever a political capital. He says it is not an exceptionally impressive hillfort (Hogg, 1975, 41), although he does concede the hypothesis is a reasonable attempt to link history with visible monuments. Llanmelin was more probably a defended enclosure for corralling. Stock, both cattle and horses, were considered valuable and determined one's standing both within and outside the clan unit.

Glossary

Beaker Phase: The name given to a distinctive pottery tradition and subsequent mortuary practice found over the whole of southern Britain. The Beaker tradition is also linked to single status barrow burials. It was once thought that the Beaker people were invading tribal groups from the Continent. However, this 'invasion' is now considered to be one of ideas rather than of peoples.

Disarticulation: A form of Neolithic burial practice in which limbs were separated from bodies before final interment. It is not clear whether the bones were first defleshed, or whether fresh corpses were dismembered. (see also Excarnation)

Excarnation: The practice of exposing corpses to the elements, perhaps on some kind of specially constructed platform. North West Coastal American Indians are among peoples known to have practised excarnation.

Forecourt: The public area in front of a tomb delineated by kerbing and horns. This area was apparently reserved for rituals involving ceremonial feasting.

Gallery Grave: A Neolithic burial monument in which the passage and burial chamber lack clear separation.

Hunter/Gatherer/Fisher: This term has been traditionally used to describe small mobile band societies such as the !Kung bushpeople of Southern Africa and earlier Mesolithic groups prior to settlement and the construction of megalithic chambered tombs. However, the term may refer to a diversity of subsistence strategies relying principally upon naturally-occurring resources rather than cultivated crops and domesticated animals. Such economies may have supported quite complex, ranked societies.

Intervisibility: A term used to indicate mutual visibility, usually between corresponding styles of monument. Intervisibility may indicate a social and political relationship between neighbouring monuments and their people.

Liminal Space: This is a transitional space through which individuals undergoing rites of passage may travel. The most obvious of these is initiation: from boyhood to manhood. But human remains may also pass through liminal space on the final journey from life to ancestor status. The long passages evident within some monuments may indicate the path taken during this ritual.

Portal Dolmen: A Neolithic burial monument usually consisting of a central burial chamber surrounded by a series of orthostats, or uprights, supporting a single capstone. The chamber is entered through a doorway, located between two orthostats. The structure was covered by an earthen or cairn mound and is considered an early Neolithic form. Occurs throughout Western Britain.

Severn-Cotswold Tradition: This refers to a group of Middle and late Neolithic tombs located in and around the Severn Valley and on the Cotswolds. Examples are also found in North and South Wales. These tombs are considered to be corporate monuments, that is a burial monument used by and/or for the whole community.

Appendix 1

Guide to the main sites in Monmouthshire

Name	Grid Ref	Site Type
Palaeolithic		
Caldicot (west)	49 86 to 50 87	Two handaxes & flint tools
Caldicot (west)	49 86	Levallois Flake
Chepstow	53 92	Flint
King Arthur's Cave (Hfds.)	546 156	Cave
Merlin's Cave (Hfds.)	556 153	Cave
St Peter's Cave	539 927	Cave
Mesolithic		
Lanbadoc Fawr	36 07	Flint
Machen Lower	23 88	Flint
Michaelstone	23 83	Petit Tranchet Axe
Usk	37 00	Flint
Neolithic		
Gaer Llwyd, Shirenewton	448 968	Chambered Tomb
Gwern y Cleppa, Duffryn	276 851	Chambered Tomb
Harold's Stones, Trelech United	499 051	Stone Alignment
Heston Brake, Portskewett	505 887	Chambered Tomb
Thornwell Farm, Chepstow	540 917	Chambered Tomb
Bronze Age		
Bedd y Gwr Hir, Llanelly	246 134	Standing Stone
Blorence Cairn, Llanfoist Fawr	270 119	Round Cairn
Caerwent	451 909	Round Barrow
Caerwent	451 909	Round Barrow
Caldicot Castle	487 886	Trackway
Caldicot Castle	487 886	Boat
Caldicot Castle	487 886	House structure
Caldicot Level, Magor	431 841	Trackway
Careg Croes-Ifor, Blaenavon	248 106	Round Cairn
Carn y Defaid, Llanfoist	271 100	Round Barrow
Carreg Maen-Taro	238 113	Standing Stone

Chapel Tump, Magor	447 851	Settlement
Crick Round Barrow, Caerwent	484 903	Round Barrow
Crucorney Fawr	290 298	Round Cairn
Crucorney Fawr	293 294	Round Cairn
Druidstone, Michaelstone	241 834	Standing Stone
Graig	258 848	Cairn
Gray Hill Complex, Caerwent	44 93	Barrow/Cairn Cemetery
Gray Hill, Caerwent	438 935	Stone Circle
Gray Hill, Caerwent	438 936	Standing Stone
Gray Hill, Caerwent	438 935	Standing Stone (recumbent)
Gray Hill, Caerwent	438 935	Standing Stone
Henllys Complex	25 92	Barrow Cemetery (5)
Lang Stone, Langstone	377 896	Standing Stone
Langstone	382 891	Round Barrow
Llanelly	213 140	Round Barrow
Llanfihangel Stone	445 878	Standing Stone
Llangattock	461 194	Round Barrow
Llangybi Stone, Llangybi Fawr	380 964	Standing Stone
Llanover Fawr	351 080	Round Barrow
Llanthony, Crucorney Fawr	28 25	Cairn Cemetery (5)
Llanvaches (Wentwood)	417 950	Round Barrow
Llanvaches (Wentwood)	417 946	Round Barrow
Lower Halewood, Tintern	521 009	Round Barrow
Machen Lower	239 888	Cairn
Mathern	496 905	Round Barrow
Middle Hendre, Llangattock	454 138	Round Barrow
Mynyddislwyn	195 998	Round Barrow
Mynyddislwyn	181 907	Round Cairn
Mynyddislwyn	184 906	Round Cairn
Newport	316 843	Burial-Inhumation
Risca	244 927	Round Cairn
Rogerstone	257 906	Round Cairn
Rogerstone	255 911	Round Barrow
Rogerstone	250 908	Round Barrow
The Upton Trackway, Magor	446 850	Trackway

Tintern	521 010	Round Barrow
Tintern	520 009	Round Barrow
Tre-Garn, Langstone	384 906	Round Cairn
Trefil Las, Tredegar	12 13	Round Barrow
Trelech United	499 013	Standing Stone
Twyn Cae-Hugh, Mynyddislwyn	174 915	Round Cairn
Twyn Pant-Teg, Machen Lower	240 889	Round Barrow
Twyn-y-Bleiddiaid, Bedwellty	186 027	Round Cairn

Iron Age

Bishop Barnet's Camp, St Arvans	520 942	Enclosure
Blackfield Wood	529 990	Hillfort
Caerau, Llanfrechfa Lower	330 934	Hillfort
Camp Hill, Llanarth Fawr	391 079	Enclosure
Castell Prin, Penhow	410 924	Hillfort
Coe Camp, Llangennock Fawr	359 939	Hillfort
Coed y Bwndd Camp, Llanarth	365 068	Hillfort
Coed y Caera, Langstone	378 915	Enclosure
Craig y Gaer, Llanelly	223 133	Hillfort
Croes-Carn-Einion, Graig	258 863	Hillfort
Gaer Hill Camp, Tintern	517 980	Hillfort
Gaer, Llanelly	225 153	Enclosure
Gaer, Trelech United	493 038	Hillfort
Great House Camp, Llangwm	432 033	Hillfort
Grosmont Fawr	389 210	Hillfort
Gwehelog Fawr	397 025	Enclosure
Kymin Hill, Monmouth	521 128	Hillfort
Llancayo Camp, Gwehelog Fawr	378 138	Hillfort
Llanddewi Sgyrrid	331 183	Hillfort
Llanmelin Wood, Caerwent	461 926	Hillfort
Lodge Wood, Caerleon	323 913	Hillfort
Lower Camp, Piercefield	533 958	Hillfort
Maindee Camp, Newport	331 886	Enclosure
Pen Twyn, Crucorney Fawr	321 230	Hillfort
Pen-Toppen-Ash, Langstone	379 915	Enclosure
Piercefield Camp, St Arvans	537 960	Hillfort
Rhiwderin Camp, Graig	264 877	Hillfort

Risca	23 90	Iron Age/Roman Mine
St Julian's Wood, Christchurch	340 892	Hillfort
Sudbrook Camp, Portskewett	506 873	Hillfort
The Bulwarks, Chepstow	538 927	Hillfort
The Larches Camp, Caerwent	433 900	Hillfort
The Mount, Graig	259 849	Hillfort
Tredegar Hillfort, Newport	290 868	Hillfort
Twm Barlwm, Risca	244 927	Hillfort
Twyn Bell Camp, Llanbadoc Fawr	375 000	Enclosure/Camp
Twyn y Gaer, Crucorney Fawr	294 220	Hillfort
Twyn yr Allt, Abergavenny	296 163	Enclosure/Hillfort
Twyn-y-Dinas, Llanelly	228 125	Hillfort
Wilcrick Hill Camp, Wilcrick	411 878	Hillfort

Bibliography

Andrews Downman, E., 1916, *Ancient Earthworks in Monmouthshire,* (unpublished)

Barber, C. & Williams, 1989, *The Ancient Stones of Wales,* Abergavenny, Blorenge Books

Barker, C.T., 1992, *The Chambered Tombs of South-West Wales: A re-assessment of the Neolithic burial monuments of Carmarthenshire and Pembrokeshire,* Oxbow Monograph 14

Barnett, C., 1964, 'A Beaker Cist at Beachley', *The Monmouthshire Antiquary,* 112-116

Barnwell, E.L., 1884, 'On some South Wales Cromlechs', *Archaeologia Cambrensis,* (5th series), 1, 129-144

Bersu, G., 1940, 'Excavations at Little Woodbury (Wiltshire), the settlement revealed by excavation', *Proceedings of the Prehistoric Society,* 6, 30-111

Boon, G.C., 1980, 'Caerleon and the Gwent Levels in early historical times', in F.H.Thompson (ed.) *Archaeology and Coastal Change,* London, Society of Antiquaries

Bourdieu, P., 1977, *Outline of a Theory of Practice,* Cambridge, Cambridge University Press

Bowra, C.M., 1962, *Primitive Song,* London, Weidenfeld and Nicolson

Bradley, R., 1984, 'Studying Monuments', in R. Bradley and J. Gardiner (eds.) *Neolithic Studies: A Review of some Current Research,* B.A.R. British Series 133, 61-66

Briggs, C.S., 1973, 'Double Axe Doubts' *Antiquity* 47, 318-320

Britnell, W.J. & Savory, H.N., 1984, *Gwernvale and Penywyrlod: Two Neolithic Long Cairns in the Black Mountains of Brecknock,* Cambrian Archaeological Monographs No.2

Burgess, C.B., 1962, 'A socketed axe from central Monmouthshire', *Mon. Ant.*, I, 17-27

Burl, A., 1977, *Stone Circles of the British Isles*

Caseldine, A., 1990, *Environmental Archaeology in Wales*, Cadw Welsh Historical Monuments & Dept. of Archaeology, St David's University College, Lampeter

Castleden, R., 1992, *Neolithic Britain: New Stone Age Sites of England, Scotland and Wales*, London, Routledge

Children, G. & Nash, G.H., 1994, *Prehistoric Sites of Herefordshire,* Logaston Press, Herefordshire

Children, G. & Nash, G.H., 1996, *Symbolic Landscapes: the Chambered Monuments of South-West Wales,* Pembrokeshire Coast National Park

Collins, P., 1965, *Changing Ideals in Modern Architecture,* London, Faber & Faber

Corcoran, J.X.W.P., 1969, 'The Cotswold-Severn Group', in T.G.E. Powell et al. *Megalithic Enquiries in the West of Britain,* 13-104, Liverpool University Press

Daniel, G.E., 1950, *The Prehistoric Chambered Tombs of England and Wales*, Cambridge University Press

Darvill, T.C., 1982, *The Megalithic Chambered Tombs of the Cotswold-Severn Region,* Vorda Research Series, No.5

Darvill, T.C., 1989, 'The Circulation of Neolithic Stone and Flint Axes: a case study from Wales and the mid-west of England', *Proceedings of the Prehistoric Society,* 55, 27-43

Davis, M., 1945, 'Types of Megalithic Monument of the Irish Sea and North Channel Coastlands: A Study of Distributions', *Antiquity*, 25, 125-144

Fried, M.H., 1975, *The Notion of Tribe*, Menlo Park, Calif., Cummings Publishing Company

Gent, G. & Dean, C., 1986, 'Catchment Analysis and Settlement Hierarchy: A case study from Pre-Roman Britain', in E. Grant (ed.) *Central Places, Archaeology and History,* University of Sheffield

Green, M., 1995, *Celtic Goddesses: Warriors, Virgins and Mothers,* London, British Museum Press

Grimes, W.F., 1932, 'Prehistoric Archaeology in Wales since 1925. The Neolithic Period', *Proceedings of the Prehistoric Society of East Anglia,* 7, 85-92

Grimes, W.F., 1936, 'The Megalithic Monuments of Wales', *Proceedings of the Prehistoric Society,* 2, 106-139

Grimes, W.F., 1951, The Prehistory of Wales, Cardiff

Harding, D.W., 1974, *The Iron Age in Lowland Britain,* London, Routledge and Kegan Paul

Harré, R., 1993, *Social Being* (2nd Edition), Oxford, Blackwell

Haselgrove, C., 1986, 'Central Places in British Iron Age Studies', in E. Grant (ed) *Central Places, Archaeology and History,* Sheffield, University of Sheffield

Hodder, I., 1990, *The Domestication of Europe*, Oxford, Blackwell

Hogg, A.H.A., 1975, *Hill Forts of Britain*

Houlder, C. H., 1978, *Wales: An Archaeological Guide*, London, Faber & Faber

Houlder, C.H., 1988, 'The Petrological Identification of Stone Implements from Wales', in T.H. Clough and W.A. Cummins (eds.) *Stone Axe Studies*, Vol 2, 133-136 & 246-260

Hugh-Jones, C., 1979, *From the Milk River*, Cambridge University Press

Huntley, B., 1990, 'European Vegetation in history: Palaeo-vegetation maps from Pollen data - 13,000 yrs B.P. to present', *Journal of Quarternary Science,* Vol 5, no.2, 183-222, Willey

Kinnes, I., 1992, *Non-Megalithic Long Barrows and Allied Structures in the British Neolithic,* British Museum Occasional Paper No.52

Lynch, F.M. & Burgess, C., (eds.), 1972, *Prehistoric Man in Wales and the West*, Bath, Adams and Dart

Nash-Williams, V.E., 1933, 'An early Iron Age Hillfort at Llanmelin', *Arch. Camb.*, 88, 237-346

Nash-Williams, V.E., 1939, 'Early Iron Age ... camp at Sudbrook', *Arch. Camb.*, 94, 42-79

Perry, V., 1994, *Built for a Better Future: The Brynmawr Rubber Factory*, Oxford, White Cockade

Piggott, S., 1975, *The Druids*, London, Thames and Hudson

Powell, T.G.E., Corcoran, J.X.W.P., Lynch, F. & Scott, J.G., 1969, *Megalithic Enquiries in the West of Britain*, Liverpool University Press

Probert, L.A., 1976, *Twyn-y-Gaer Hillfort, Gwent: an interim assessment*, Archaeology of Wales

Rees, T., 1815, *A Topographical and Historical Description of South Wales*, London, Sherwood, Neely and Jones

Ross, A., 1967, *Pagan Celtic Britain*, London, Cardinal

Savory, H.N., 1980, 'The Neolithic in Wales', in J.A.Taylor (ed.) *Culture and Environment in Prehistoric Wales*, British Archaeological Report No.76, Oxford, 207-232

Service, E.R., 1962, *Primitive Social Organisation: an evolutionary perspective*, New York, Random House

Simmons, I. & Tooley, M., 1981, *The Environment of British Prehistory*, Duckworth

Stanford, S.C., 1991, *The Archaeology of The Welsh Marches*, (2nd Ed.) S.C.Stanford, 2-73

Thomas, J., 1990, *Rethinking the Neolithic*, Cambridge, Cambridge University Press

Tilley, C., 1994, *A Phenomenology of Landscape: Paths, Places and Monuments*, London, Berg

Trigger, B., 1978, 'Ethnoarchaeology: Some Cautionary Considerations', in E. Tooker (ed) *Ethnology by Archaeologists*, 1978 Proceedings of the American Ethnological Society, Washington, AES

Walters, B., 1992, *The Archaeology and History of Ancient Dean and the Wye Valley*, 8- 31, Thornhill Press

Williams, A.H., 1941, *An Introduction to the History of Wales*, Vol 1, Cardiff, University of Wales Press

Wymer, J.J., 1977, *Gazetteer of Mesolithic sites in England and Wales*, Council for British Archaeology, Research Report No.22

Recent books from Logaston Press

Owain Glyn Dŵr
The War of Independence in the Welsh borders

by Geoffrey Hodges, this book concentrates on the background to and the actual fighting in the borders. The tensions leading up to the revolt are considered, as are the politics of early fifteenth century England and Wales. The battles of Pilleth and Hyddgen are examined in detail, as is the Franco-Welsh advance on Worcester. Finally the evidence is detailed for Owain spending his last days with his daughters in Herefordshire. 256pp with photographs. £9.95 ISBN 1 873827 24 5

The Civil War in Hereford

by Ron Shoesmith. Documents from the Civil War are used to tell the history of the four sieges by Parliament of Hereford together with the accompanying strife in the county as a whole. Ironically the best prepared army led by one of the most experienced generals of the age, that of the Scots led by Alexander Leslie, Earl of Leven, was the one which failed with much loss of life. Two earlier attempts succeeded after brief skirmishes, with resultant court martials for some of the Royalist officers; the final attempt resulted in a pamphlet entitled *A new tricke to take Townes*. 176pp with maps and photographs. £8.95 ISBN 1 873827 34 2

A View from Hereford's Past

by Richard Stone and Nic Appleton-Fox, this tells of the excavation of the precincts of Hereford Cathedral in preparation for the building of the new Mappa Mundi exhibition centre. It relates several surprising finds, including over 1,100 complete skeletons and charnel of an additional 5,000 bodies. The excavation has also shed new light on the road layout and style of buildings of the Saxon city; of the diseases that prevailed amongst the medieval population and much besides. Whilst serving as the interim archaeological report, the text is written in a way that anyone interested in finding out in substantial detail what has so far emerged from the archaeological work can do so. 80pp with 44 photographs, maps and illustrations. (A4 format, bound) £9.95 ISBN 1 873827 39 3

Other books in the Monuments in the Landscape series

Vol. 1 Prehistoric Sites of Herefordshire

by George Children and George Nash, this is similar in format and style to the *Prehistoric Sites of Monmouthshire*. Herefordshire is well-known for its array of hillforts, and many of these are detailed in the site descriptions, together with earlier barrows, standing stones and chambered tombs. 144pp with some 50 photographs, plans and maps. £6.95. ISBN 1 873827 09 1

Vol. II Castles & Moated Sites of Herefordshire

by Ron Shoesmith. Herefordshire is a county of castles and moated sites, reflecting its position as a well populated agricultural county bordering disputed territory. The history of defence within the county is explained, as is that of castle building, their use and, finally, demise. There is a comprehensive gazetteer of all the sites set out parish by parish with much recent information. 256pp with some 65 photographs, plans and maps. £9.95. ISBN 1 873827 59 8

Vol. III Castles of Radnorshire

by Paul Remfry. The history of the centuries of warfare and changing alliances in Radnorshire is covered in some detail for it provides the background to the construction of the castles; indeed, much of the recorded history is about the regular sieges and their capture. Detailed information is also given about all the castle sites. 160pp with some 35 photographs, plans and maps. £7.95. ISBN 1 873827 54 7